Endorse

"Every generation needs to learn the same wisdom their predecessors had to learn in order to succeed. The trouble is, it is usually communicated in the way the previous generation learned it and so the new folks reject it as out of date, at their own peril. Robert Terson has captured not only the sales wisdom of the ages but also the storytelling mastery of the great teachers and brought it together for you in *Selling Fearlessly*. This is a book you will remember. It is filled with vivid, compelling stories, told in a personal style that makes you a part of the action. Enjoy this book and then assure that your colleagues and later, your kids, read it too."

Jim Cathcart, Author of *Relationship Selling*

"Wow! This book is overloaded with practical methods and techniques you can use immediately to get more prospects, make better presentations, and close more sales."

Brian Tracy, Author of *The Psychology of Selling*

"A treasure trove of valuable sales information in an extremely readable book. Selling Fearlessly should be required reading for anybody in sales or customer service, whether they have one year or 40 years of experience."

Dr. Tony Alessandra, Author of 27 business books including *Non-Manipulative Selling* and *The Platinum Rule*

"Selling is a shared experience that salespeople have all by themselves. If you think that selling is scary or something you just aren't cut out for, read Selling Fearlessly. Gain from Bob Terson's 40 years of been-there-done-that experience. You'll quickly discover you aren't alone and that the path you're on leads to happy customers and success."

Chris Lytle, Author of *The Accidental Salesperson* and *The Accidental Sales Manager*

"In *Selling Fearlessly* Robert Terson presents one of the most useful presentations on selling that you'll ever read. You won't find great, deep, highly sophisticate—and useless—discussions of sales theory found in so many 'serious' sales books, nor will you find the silly—and meaningless—platitudes found in many "motivational" sales books. Instead you'll find a great storyteller who relates real world experiences—and lessons learned—in selling over a long and highly successful career. Read and pay attention, for this is the real world of selling—and there are real lessons that all successful sellers must learn. You can learn them from Terson, or you can learn them the hard way on the street. Your choice."

Paul McCord, Sales Trainer/Consultant and best-selling author

"With *Selling Fearlessly*, Bob Terson has taken us into the world of the 'real' salesperson where we get to experience his frustrations, lessons learned, tricks and tips and keys to success. Most important, we get the inside secrets that only someone with Bob's background and insight could share. With 40+ years of experience, Bob has seen it all and his book is an exceptional guide and truly 'A Master Salesman's Instructional Manual.' Filled with stories and great examples (e.g., let's all start selling like Andy the iPad® guy), *Selling Fearlessly* is a book to be read multiple times—for some great reminders, humorous commentary, and sales inspiration."

Sam Richter, CEO/Founder SBR Worldwide/Know More!
Best-Selling Author of *Take the Cold Out of Cold Calling*

"If you're in sales—and we're all in sales—read Robert Terson's *Selling Fearlessly*. It's not only entertaining but it's packed full of information that anyone who ever wants to sell anything to anyone else needs to know. If this book doesn't pay for itself many times over, you simply weren't paying attention and you need to read it again."

Barry Maher, Author of *No Lie: Truth is the Ultimate Sales Tool!*

"There are a ton of sales books out there; but this one addresses *all* the elements of selling, broken down in three key areas—Mental Attitude, Work Habits, and Salesmanship. Terson doesn't just *tell* you how to sell, he *shows* you how; you'll be entertained as much as enlightened by a master storyteller with 43 years of in-the-trenches selling experience. *Selling Fearlessly* is perfectly suited for all types of selling but will have most value to the one-call-close salesperson. Curl up and enjoy!"

Daniel Adams, Principal: Adams & Associates, Author of *Building Trust, Growing Sales,* Developer of Trust Triangle Selling™ Workshops and The Sales Strategizer™ iPhone App

"*Selling Fearlessly* is just that, giving great insight into how to sell fearlessly from a successful salesman that proved it works for over 40 years! With great stories Robert Terson goes to the heart of the matter and demonstrates what it really takes to be on top. If you're looking for a quick fix, easy street or a magic bullet, this is not the place. On the other hand if you want real consistent success in selling, *Selling Fearlessly* shows you the way. The stories are captivating and pointed, an easy read yet with plenty of meat to push your sales to another level consistently."

Harlan Goerger, President AskHG.com,
Three times Business Author; Sales Trainer & Coach

"In sales, it really is experience that counts. Bob Terson shares what he has learned and shows you what works. His 40+ years in sales and business will help you cut the learning curve and improve your sales closing ratio immediately. Great reading for beginners and old pros alike, use his book as a reference guide to your future success."

Brian Bieler, Author of *The Sales Operator*

"With hesitancy, I picked up yet another sales related book and much to my delight was swept away by pages whose fragrance was reminiscent of the legendary Ziglar. Bob's sincerity shines through not as advice, but as inspiration; well worth the read! Women, you'll enjoy listening to a man who speaks from the heart, neither patronizing nor condescending in any way."

Terri Dunevant, Award-Winning Author of *The Staircase Principle*

"Robert Terson takes his more than 40 years of selling experience and offers us a book that is compelling! A hard hitting 'how to' book on selling, these pages are full of engaging stories and specific techniques you can use in each step of the sales process. Whether it be closing techniques or what to do after the sale, his advice is excellent for the new salesperson and the seasoned expert. Don't just read *Selling Fearlessly*—use it as a hands-on tool!"

Mark Hunter, "The Sales Hunter," Author of *High-Profit Selling: Win the Sale Without Compromising on Price*

"Over the decades that have passed since my friend, Bob Terson, started selling, a lot of things have changed. But what hasn't changed is captured neatly in Bob's book, be it the ability to tell a story (and Bob has plenty), the mental attitude that leads to success, the work ethic required to succeed and win, or mastering the fundamentals of selling. Pick up *Selling Fearlessly* and join Bob on a wild ride through the world of selling—and sell fearlessly on the other side!"

Anthony Iannarino, Author of *The Sales Blog* at www.thesalesblog.com

"The one must have attribute to successful selling is confidence. Confidence in yourself, your company, the products and services you're selling and the pricing structure are imperative. In a very personal book that every salesperson can relate to, you will learn through Bob Terson's colorful, real life experiences how to become a fearless seller."

Gary Hart, Four decades of sales and marketing success

Presenting to Donald Trump

Barry Thalden once told me a great story about presenting to Donald Trump: "I managed to arrange a meeting with Donald Trump. We met in what later became the infamous Board Room on his TV show *The Apprentice*. My presentation was on slides. As I started to set up my projector, he immediately objected. Undaunted, I told him it would only take a few minutes and would fully explain the opportunity I'd come to show him. Once the presentation began he interrupted me several times, trying to rush me along; each time I told him I was just getting to the part he wanted to know about. I'd come all the way to New York to see him; I was going to do it my way, come hell or high water. I wasn't going to chicken out, be intimidated because he was Donald Trump. When the presentation was over he said, 'I can't believe you got me to sit through your entire presentation—my rule for meetings is 12 minutes and out.' As you know, I got the job." If Thalden can stand his ground with an egomaniac like Trump, you can do the same with anyone—*if*, like Thalden, you're fearless.

SELLING FEARLESSLY

A MASTER SALESMAN'S SECRETS FOR THE ONE-CALL-CLOSE SALESPERSON

ROBERT TERSON

Winthrop & Foster Publishing
Chicago, Illinois

SELLING FEARLESSLY
A Master Salesman's Secrets for the One-Call-Close Salesperson

Robert Terson

Winthrop & Foster Publishing
Chicago, Illinois

Robert@sellingfearlessly.com
www.sellingfearlessly.com

Cover Design: Jason Witt
Interior Layout: www.TheBookProducer.com

Printed in the United States of America

Library of Congress Control Number: 2012947228
ISBN: 978-0-9881823-0-1

For Barry Thalden, who wouldn't
take no for an answer.

Acknowledgments

You don't write a book about selling, after a 40-plus-year career as a sales professional, without realizing it never could have happened without the support, teaching, urging, and good will provided by so many individuals, including some I've never had the pleasure of meeting and knowing. It's impossible to acknowledge them all, especially *all* the authors of the countless books I've benefited from throughout my life, but I do want to say thank you to many of those who have markedly influenced my professional life and directly influenced the creation of the book you now hold in your hands.

Five special authors: Napoleon Hill, author of *Think and Grow Rich*—no book has meant more to my professional success, happiness in life. Frank Bettger, author of *How I Raised Myself from Failure to Success in Selling*—my favorite sales book. Zig Ziglar, author of multiple sales books, including *Zig Ziglar's Secrets of Closing the Sale,* and the best speaker/philosopher I ever listened to. John Braine, author of *Writing a Novel*, the best book on writing fiction I ever read. William Strunk, Jr., author of *The Elements of Style*, which provides the essence of good writing, without all the hoopla.

The sales and marketing writers who graciously took the time to read my book and then were kind enough to endorse it: Jay Conrad Levinson, Brian Tracy, Tom Hopkins, Jim Cathcart, Barry Maher, Daniel Adams, Harlan Goerger, Brian Bieler, Terri Dunevant, Paul McCord, Sam Richter, Dave Kurlan, Jill Konrath, Chris Lytle, Mark Hunter, Anthony Iannarino, Gary Hart, and Dr. Tony Alessandra. I especially want to thank Chris Lytle, who became a good friend and mentor; no author more positively influenced the rewrite than Chris—I owe him Big Time! Dr. Alessandra, too, went way out of his busy way for me by writing the foreword to *Selling Fearlessly.*

Judy Slack, who works with Tom Hopkins. Her many kindnesses conceivably could reach the top of Mount Everest.

Bob Burg, who also went way out of his way for me and showed me what a great speaker is all about.

Three friends and my primary physician, who read the first draft that I was comfortable enough to let anyone see, and provided invaluable feedback: Greg Scherzinger, Roger Bosworth, Barry Thalden, and Dr. Robert Zimmanck. It was Barry Thalden who, for over 25 years, urged me to write a book about selling. I didn't want to; he said I *had* to; he was right. In so many ways it's his book, which is why it's dedicated to him.

The salespeople I worked for before I went into business for myself: Lowell Martin, Harry Rabin, and Bob Trudeau; it was Trudeau who taught me the telephone-book-cover advertising business and self-discipline.

All the people who ever bought from me, put their faith in me, honored me with their trust.

Jason Witt, who designed my website and the front cover of this book. Anyone who has the opportunity to do business with this marvelously talented young man should jump at the chance to do so!

Janet S. Mowery, who did a masterful job of editing the final manuscript.

The hundreds of friends I've made on Twitter, LinkedIn, and Facebook, especially the members of North America's Best, the mastermind sales group I'm so honored to be part of: Miles Austin, Karin Bellantoni, Cara Celli, Jim Domanski, Terri Dunevant, Matt Goff, Charles H. Green, Gary Hart, Lynn Hidy, Leanne Hoagland Smith, Mark Hunter, Anthony Iannarino, Jim Keenan, Jerry Kennedy, Mike Kunkle, Alen Mayer, Paul McCord, Kelly McCormick, Nancy Nardin, Andy Paul, Don F. Perkins, Doug Rice, Lori Richardson, Kelly Riggs, Kelley Robertson, Steven Rosen, Richard Ruff, Todd Schnick, Tibor Shanto, Elinor Stutz, Babette N. Ten Haken, Ken Thoreson, Dan Waldschmidt, and Mike Weinberg.

Peter Notschke, who has become a good friend and my technology mentor; I'd be lost without him.

Richard Fenton and Andrea Waltz, whose input regarding the publishing of this book has been invaluable.

My late father, Al Terson—my sales consigliore; the man who taught me more about selling than everyone else put together.

My incomparable wife, Nicki, and my three children—Michael (Nicole), Jacob (Julie), and Jessi. My three grandchildren—Jazmine, Jack, and Jordana. My brother Harlan and my sister-in-law Kris. My sister-in-law Diane and brother-in-law Steve. My friend and accountant, Dave Levinson—a second brother. No man ever had a stronger, more supportive family.

All my other friends, without whom life would be a bore, especially Stu Pearl and Ron Treiber.

Finally, all of you. What is a writer without an audience? I pray my efforts prove worthy of the vision I had when I sat down to write this book; that they enlighten, inspire, and entertain you; that they make you a stronger salesperson and put a lot of money in your pocket.

Contents

Foreword
By Dr. Tony Alessandra

These are questions few people have asked before:

- Are salespeople afraid of some or all of their prospects?
- Do they see themselves as subservient to their prospects?
- Do they suffer from acute fear of failure?
- Is fear the number one reason for their lack of success?

Are these questions especially pertinent to the 80% of salespeople who only do 20% of the business?

If you were to do a survey asking 500 salespeople what their greatest fears are, chances are you would get a lot of surprised looks and statements along the lines of "I'm not afraid of anything." Chances are, too, the salespeople may not be lying to you; they may really believe to be true what they said. The reason for that is "fear" is not an emotion most of us are consciously in touch with or, even if we are, we hate to admit it. It's just too painful and embarrassing and, too often, an invitation to ridicule from one's peers. It is a vast conspiracy really—a king-sized barrier to successful selling—to even discuss it, let alone confront it, is a taboo most refuse to confront.

In *Selling Fearlessly*, Bob Terson confronts this mighty taboo for all of us and we are all the better off for it; for to be successful in selling requires challenging our fears and forever banishing them to a locked closet and throwing away the key.

Those of us who are true professionals call on people to help them, serve them, better their business lives. We are not there to manipulate or exploit them for our own benefit. To perform at the highest levels, we cannot be afraid of them. Why should we? To perform at the highest levels, we must be the equal of our prospects and customers and why shouldn't we? Again, we are professionals, are we not? Do we not deserve their respect and even gratitude for the excellent work we do on their behalf? Absolutely! Fear, like all emotions, is simply a state of mind—a *temporary* state of mind. If you are willing to look deep within yourself, confront and challenge your fears, slash your way through them, success beyond your wildest imagination awaits you.

Selling Fearlessly is not only a hands-on tool to get you past your fears, it will *show* you how to sell from the perspective of a master salesperson who spent 43 years in the field selling to the same tough customers you deal with every day of your life. This book covers it all—mental attitude, work habits, salesmanship. There are elements of selling Terson brings to your attention that you have never even thought about. This is a book of stories, a book of solid, subtle technique, not a book of abstract theory. This is the *real* world of selling, a life changer, and after you've read this book, you'll never be the same or think about the sales process the same. Whether you're a newcomer or a seasoned professional, you'll find ideas in this book that will take your sales to new levels. As you put these ideas into practice, you'll see your success with customers soar. Enjoy! Greatness awaits you.

Introduction

One of my dearest friends, Barry Thalden, has exhorted me to write this book for 25 years. Thalden is an architect; his firm, Thalden, Boyd, Emery Architects—Las Vegas, St. Louis, Tulsa, Phoenix—has been designing prodigious buildings in the spirit of Ayn Rand's Howard Roark since 1972. If you've ever been in The Venetian Resort-Hotel-Casino in Las Vegas, you've seen their incredible artistry on display: Thalden, Boyd, Emery Architects provided the detailed technical drawings for the interior and exterior themed facades that make it look like Venice.

We've been friends for 52 years now, a half-century, and we've talked about selling more times than Bobby Cox got thrown out of baseball games. Thalden speaks to architects about the business side of running an architectural firm, especially the importance of selling themselves to prospective clients. For decades the subject of selling has fascinated us both, and we've both read everything about selling we could lay our hands on.

Our favorite selling book is Frank Bettger's *How I Raised Myself from Failure to Success in Selling*. Published in 1947, it's as apropos today as the day it was written; I recommend it every chance I get. What makes it such a captivating read is that Bettger *shows* how to sell through his personal stories—reading them is like watching role-playing. Thalden once told me that Bettger's book, which he read in his early 30s, was, in a *business* sense, a key inspiration for his success as an architect: "I went out and applied the principles Bettger talked about and projects started coming our way like never before, it was amazing. That book changed my business life."

"You could do that and more for people," he'd say, "I know you can; and the same way Bettger did—with all those phenomenal stories you've told me over the years—so the average guy can comprehend and apply it to change *his* life, the way Bettger changed mine. How many times have you told me there's never been a sales book—even Bettger's—that addresses *all* the elements of selling, especially the all-important fear factor that 80% of salespeople who only do 20% of the business must face every time they make a call or give a presentation? Maybe you won't invent the wheel, but you and I both know you've got something to say and are itching to say it."

I heard this theme multiple times a year for, as I said, 25 years. I'll admit it; he was sure right about the itch.

So, now that I've retired from my telephone-book-cover advertising business, after spending my entire adult life as a salesman/businessman, 43 years, it's time to follow my friend's advice and share with you all that I've learned in what has been my vocation *and* avocation. I pray that what I've created meets Barry Thalden's hopes and expectations…and most important, yours.

In my early 20s, I sold residential real estate for three fearful, undisciplined years—alas, not all that successfully. Trust me, "fearful" and "undisciplined" do not lead to "success." I recall selling a house to a man who, *after the contract was accepted*, repeatedly pushed for additional concessions from the seller; he was totally out of line, but I was so fearful of losing the sale that I gave in to him each time. Two years later I was taught to sell fearlessly and emphatically would have said no to his outrageous demands. When a salesperson can walk away from a bad deal or an abusive customer, the balance of power shifts in favor of the salesperson. The same thing happens when he overcomes the terrible fear of not making enough money to provide for his family, of not living up to his vision of success.

When my short-lived real estate career ended, I spent the next 40 years fearlessly selling advertising on telephone-book-covers to hard-nosed businesspeople (to those of you who are younger than 40, before the Internet, yellow-page directories were relevant). It was a one-call-close, "simple" (low-dollar-amount) sale. And although most of the selling elements in *Selling Fearlessly* apply to all salespeople, they are primarily directed towards the one-call-close, simple-sale salesperson. For salespeople making multiple calls to close complex (high-dollar-amount) sales to buying teams, I recommend Neil Rackham's *SPIN Selling*, which makes the important distinction between simple and complex sales.

That said, I'll ask your forgiveness for my oft use of sports analogies (I am a passionate sports buff) and ubiquitous use of the pronoun "I." But I rely on my personal selling experiences the same way Frank Bettger did. It's what I know and my best chance to make *Selling Fearlessly* come alive for you. I know this can be interpreted as ego, boasting, and no one likes a braggart. I pledge to you, my purpose is not ego. My purpose is to enlighten and inspire you—to enlighten and inspire you to become a salesperson, or be a far better salesperson than you are now. To inspire you to be that ordinary man or woman who does extraordinary things. The Reverend Bob Richards, Olympic Gold-medalist pole-vaulter in 1952 and 1956, said, "Every day ordinary people do extraordinary things." You have it within you to do extraordinary things, and the selling profession is a wondrous arena to do it in.

Selling Fearlessly truly is a salesman's instructional manual down to the grayest subtleties, some never before touched upon in a selling book, like "The Mound Road Story"; "The Devil's Retirement Story"; "Saturation Point"; "Setting the Stage"; "Telling Clues"; "The Importance of Equality"; and "The Sixth Sense." As I write this in 2012, we're in the midst of the Great Recession, and unemployment is brutalizing millions; but a plethora of sales jobs go unfilled. I say let's fill them. Let's strike a coup de grâce against unemployment, and while we're at it, let's turn some ordinary people into extraordinary salespeople. Let's change some lives for the better.

With a cup of coffee in my hand: here's to learning how to sell fearlessly.

PART I

BRIDGE TO THE TRIANGLE

1
The Mound Road Story

"I think a hero is an ordinary individual who finds strength to persevere and endure in spite of overwhelming obstacles."

Christopher Reeve (1952–2004)

In the Introduction I quoted Olympic pole-vaulter Bob Richards: "Every day ordinary people do extraordinary things." Now I'm going to tell you about an extraordinary event, 43 years ago, that turned my life around forever; I call it "The Mound Road Story." It encompasses all three sides of the selling Triangle (see Chapter 9, "The Triangle"). I've told this true story maybe a hundred times; and each time I tell it, a tidal wave of incredulity sweeps me out to sea and I ask myself: Would my professional life have been markedly different, would the success I achieved have been lessened, if that remarkable event had never taken place? It truly makes me wonder.

Here's some background to help you appreciate that improbable night and morning early in my selling career. I trained four weeks before going into the field alone on a Wednesday; my first town was New Lenox, Illinois, approximately ten miles east of Joliet. I lost two presentations that first day and two more the following day, Thursday. I also set up an appointment Thursday to present to two women, partners in a beauty salon; forty-three years have faded their names into oblivion, but we'll call them Margaret and Joanna. They were in their mid-30s and, as I recall, quite attractive. So I was 0 for 4, a bit shaky mental-attitude-wise; my fantasies had foreseen *instant* record-breaking numbers, and a dark shadow of desperation stalked me as I drove over to that beauty salon.

Bob Trudeau, who taught me the telephone-book-cover advertising business, used to say, "The first olive out of the bottle is the toughest; they start pouring out after you get that first one out." I craved that first olive out of the bottle.

My subconscious must have been working in overdrive, because when I got there, I re-qualified them to make sure they were the sole decision makers; it's a good thing I did.

"Well, actually," Margaret said, "we'd have to get our husbands' approval, too; it takes all four of us to decide anything."

The sound you would have heard was air exploding from my lungs via my agape mouth. You've heard about the deer caught frozen in the headlights? Well, that was me. I thought I'd properly qualified them earlier, but obviously not—a rookie mistake. I was making too many of them. *Oh, God, what else can go wrong?*

"Is it possible to set up a time when I can show the program to all four of you?" I asked, thinking dejectedly about the long drive home to Skokie; the long, blank drive home. It was going to be excruciating to tell my wife, Trudeau, and new colleagues that I still was a "virgin."

Joanna said, "I don't know when we could do it; they're really never here."

"No," Margaret added, "they both work at the plant. They don't get off until seven most nights—"

And then she threw me a lifeline.

"—in fact, we scheduled our monthly business meeting for tonight, right after they get off."

Oh? I gave it a shot—I boldly asked if I could give my presentation at their meeting. Was I clutching at straws? To put it mildly.

They looked somewhat dumbfounded at each other; Joanna hesitatingly said, "I guess…"

"I think it might be okay," Margaret said, "advertising is something we're planning to discuss; I don't think the guys would mind."

All right!

It was decided: after they closed the shop in about 45 minutes, I'd follow them—each had her own car—all the way to Joliet to Margaret's house, which she mentioned was on Mound Road. I left to get a cup of coffee, called my wife to let her know what her screwy husband was doing, ditto Trudeau, and anxiously waited for the time to pass. I wouldn't get home until God knows what ridiculous hour, *but I wanted that first sale.*

Setback One

When I got back to the beauty salon, my heart sank down to my toes, because the shop was closed—lights out, door locked, Margaret and Joanna gone. They'd left without me. All I had now was their business cards and an empty promise of a presentation, which unfortunately wasn't going to take place tonight.

I doubt I was ever more discouraged (well, not for another 23 years anyway, but that's another story). I dragged my jilted body and soul back to the car and got onto I-80 heading east. I screamed a litany of curses; it didn't help. I told myself it didn't matter—I'd come out swinging tomorrow; that didn't help either.

There was a bitter taste in my mouth, an aching in my gut; I wanted to punch out a wall.

I'd driven about five miles when suddenly I yelled out, "*Damn it!*" and, my heart racing, spun off at the next exit, circled around heading west towards Joliet. I was not going to give up this easily. No, sir!

You're nuts, Robert, you're absolutely nuts. You know that? WHAT ARE YOU DOING?

I was forging ahead with aggressive ignorance, that's what I was doing.

I exited at the first Joliet off-ramp, looked for a gas station to get directions to Mound Road—cell phones and GPS systems didn't exist in those days. There were none in sight, but I spotted a tavern and thought, *What the hell, why not?*

It was so dark in that gin mill I could barely make out the two patrons at the bar nursing their drinks. On the jukebox Elvis was singing "Don't." Was God was trying to tell me something? I asked the bartender if he knew where Mound Road was. He gave me a strange look, said, "Sure," and proceeded to give me directions, which I easily memorized. Luckily it wasn't far. Before I left, I used the payphone to call the home number on Margaret's card, but there was no answer.

Setback Two

It took less than five minutes to get to Mound Road, but when I did I was taken aback. Now I knew why the bartender had given me that weird look. It was a dirt road heading nowhere in the pitch-black moonless night, pockmarked with shadowy silhouettes of impoverished shanties. There was *no way* Margaret lived around here, not a chance in hell. This was one step above skid row. What in God's name was going on here?

With the aid of a flashlight I tried to catch an address on one of the shanties; the number was nowhere near Margaret's address. Well that was no surprise. This was nuts. Get me out of here.

Disaster Strikes

Suddenly I heard a loud POP and the car went deader than a slab of granite.

For a second I thought maybe someone had fired a shot at me, but when I yanked open the door to generate some light, I saw a pool of liquid rapidly spreading out around and under the car.

Oh my God!

I slammed the door shut, cried out, "Please, God, get me out of here; if you'll get me out of here right now and get me home, safe and sound, I promise I'll never do anything so utterly stupid and idiotic the rest of my life. I promise!"

What am I gonna do? I am so screwed. Oh, dear God, please help me. I was so angry with myself I could've ripped my arms from their sockets: I could have been halfway home by now—safe, warm; instead I was here, on a miserable dirt road, in the black hole of hell, in a dead car, helpless, *totally helpless*. What was so bloody damn important about one lousy sale? What could I have been *thinking*?

I sat there for about five minutes feeling sorry for myself before sanity kicked in. Flashlight in hand, I made my way to the shanty that had provided the address and knocked on the door. A tall, gaunt man greeted me with "Howdy," and I rattled off my terrible misfortune. I begged to use his telephone to call the motor club.

Please, let him have a telephone.

"'Course ya kin," he said, sounding like a recent arrival from West Virginia or Kentucky. He stepped aside, said, "Y'all come awn in, please."

Never in my life had I seen such poverty, not this up close. These were poor people, barely subsisting. In the tiny bedroom off to the left, there was a young boy and girl huddled together in a twin bed; they were staring wide-eyed at me through the open doorway. They reminded me of the cartoon characters in *Little Orphan Annie*. The entire shack could not have been more than 750 square feet, the dilapidated, ink-stained sofa and mahogany rocker from Goodwill maybe. A smell of bacon hung in the air.

I profusely thanked the man and his wife and asked where the telephone was. He said, "Ya know, Ah'm purdy good with cars; how 'bout ya lemme take a peek at 'er; mebbe I kin do somethin'; no harm'n tryin', right?"

I probably embarrassed the man, the way I thanked him over and over again. I never was more grateful to receive aid from anyone. I handed him the keys and flashlight, and he ventured out to see what miracles he could perform.

I plopped down on the sofa and prayed anxiously.

The wife offered me a glass of water, which I accepted; what I really could have used was a straight bourbon, but I wasn't about to ask. We exchanged a few pleasantries but mostly sat there in dumb silence.

He was gone about ten minutes—an eternity. When he finally returned he grinned, said, "Ya in luck, mah friend; 'taint nothin' but a water hose come undone from the radiator. I'll just git 'er tightened a bit, fill 'er with some water and she'll be all fixed like new. Y'all'll be on yer way in no time a'tall."

I could have hugged that wonderful Good Samaritan, his wife, too. I owed them big-time, truly I did. They may not have been educated, or have much materially, but they were what my father liked to call "a Class Act." On this night they were a godsend.

While he repaired my car, I called Margaret again; this time she picked up on the first ring. She was astonished to hear from me. It turns out she and Joanna had done an Alphonse-Gaston act: Margaret had been parked in front, Joanna in back, behind the shop; each drove off thinking I was following the other. After arriving at Margaret's house, which was on a different Mound Road across town, they were shocked to discover how mistaken they were.

I gave her a quick rundown of my adventure on the dirt Mound Road; she apologized for the mix-up, asked if I still wanted to give them the presentation. The guys would be there around 7:45.

You bet, I told her, and used my pocket secretary to write down the directions.

Okay, let's do this.

I tried to give my Good Samaritan some cash, but he waved me off, wouldn't hear of it. "Jus' glad to help ya," he said. The next day I sent him a fifty, with no return address so he couldn't send it back.

The Other Mound Road

Margaret's house was a two-story structure in a rather classy neighborhood. The women greeted me enthusiastically, apologized again for the screw-up; they were so sorry.

Not to worry, I told them, all's well that ends well. I had no idea how premature I was, because that's when they hit me with the bad news, as if I needed more bad news.

"The guys just called," Margaret said; "there's an emergency at the plant and it looks like they're not getting off until 11:30 now, probably won't get here until after midnight." She was so sorry. "So sorry," was beginning to sound like a recording; I wanted to *scream*.

Margaret asked, "What do you want to do?"

How about shoot myself. I felt like Job.

"Do you mind if I wait?" In for a penny, in for a pound, my mother, famous for her aphorisms, used to say.

"No, of course not," Margaret said.

Joanna added, "We hoped you would."

So I waited, from 7:15 to 12:15. I could bore you with what went on during those interminable five hours, but I'll be kind.

When the husbands finally arrived, they were not thrilled to see me, got angry when they found out why I was there; incredibly, their wives had not told them I'd be there. They'd had a tough night and the last thing they needed was a "damn lousy salesman" giving them a "damn lousy presentation" about some "damn lousy advertising." I had to use every ounce of persuasion I could come up with simply to get them to listen for a few minutes. I promised, if at any point they didn't like what they heard, I'd shut up and leave.

Phew!

Maybe I should have opted for an academic career.

The average presentation in those days was about an hour and twenty minutes; this one took *three and a half hours*, I kid you not. Remember, I had *four* people asking questions and firing objections at me; for the first hour, the guys hostile as Yosemite Sam.

I walked out of there at 3:45 in the morning.

With my first sale tucked safely away in my jacket breast pocket, over my gleeful pounding heart.

The dollar volume was $463.16.

Not much compared to the huge sales I brought in years later, but it was, and still is, *the* most satisfying sale I ever closed.

Euphoria

I drove home but could have flapped my arms and flown all the way.

Euphoric, that's what I was. There was no drug on earth that could match the high engulfing me. I had done it. I had withstood every roadblock the gods had strewn across my path...and was Victorious.

Trudeau was blown away. He followed up the sale for me (I slept all day Friday), and reportedly Margaret asked him, "Did he tell you what time he left our house?" My colleagues had a newfound respect for me. I later found out all four had warned Trudeau not to hire me. Why? My weak handshake. Never again did I shake a hand without giving a firm, worthy squeeze.

Trudeau suggested I take the positive feelings from my extraordinary experience and store them in a "jug" for safekeeping, so when things weren't going so well, when I needed a lift, I could take a swig from that jug to lift my spirits. It was great advice.

If I truly am the man I was that fateful night and morning, then I'm always that man, true?

You're darn right it's true.

If you haven't experienced it already, somewhere along the way you'll have your own extraordinary story to tell, and won't that be something? Until you do, please, borrow the jug and take a swig on me whenever you need one; and remember—it's overcoming those "insurmountable" hurdles that make a salesperson strong and sets the tone for an entire career.

2

We're All Salespeople

"Everyone lives by selling something."

Robert Louis Stevenson (1850-1894)

My younger son, Jake, would tell you that, unlike his father, he could never be a salesman; he would tell you this with the same conviction he has that the sun rises in the east and sets in the west. He sees it as an unyielding Absolute, so sure is he. And, of course, he's not alone—millions share this belief with Jake. Have your livelihood depend on standing in front of an endless succession of total strangers, some downright hostile, to persuade them to *buy* something? Are you kidding! Uh-uh, no thank you! They would rather swim from Cuba to Haiti in shark-infested waters, even the ones who can't swim. Just the thought of having to make a living selling makes them tremble and sweat like a condemned black-hooded prisoner atop the gallows.

Never mind that, one way or another, they're all selling every day of their lives: to get their point across, to get what they want from their fellow man, and in some cases, just to survive. That they do not, cannot, sell is a myth, which they have (that's right...) sold to themselves.

The Mouse

I have a penchant for giving people nicknames based on their appearance, character, and especially behavior. Over two decades ago, before Nicki and I built our house in Arlington Heights, we lived in a condominium. In fact, I did two stints as president of that 28-unit building. In one of those apartments lived a fascinating elderly couple—Leo the Lion and his wife the Mouse. They've both since passed away.

I called him Leo the Lion, the king of beasts, because he was a boisterous, aggressive, know-it-all, who never hesitated to render his opinion, no matter the topic being discussed, usually in the form of a roar; never was there a perceived injustice that "Leo" wouldn't sink his teeth into, and if he got really upset, he would brandish his cane in your face like a sword.

The king's wife, the Mouse, was his direct opposite in demeanor and excitability. She was a tiny, meek woman, shy as a church mouse, who said little, always trailing two steps behind her lord and master. In nine years I never once heard the Mouse criticize or contradict her husband, or display any normal wifely disapproval of him. I would have knelt at his feet to take lessons on *that* point (just kidding). She wore nondescript clothing, not a hint of flair or élan. If not for her plain looks and dress, she would have made the perfect Stepford wife.

It happened that "Leo" was hospitalized at Lutheran General Hospital, where my wife has worked for over 32 years. Lutheran General was three-quarters of a mile from our building. One rainy late afternoon in April, Nicki and I encountered the Mouse going up in the elevator. Obviously distressed, she blurted out what had befallen poor "Leo"—a minor stroke—then stepped out onto the fourth floor with us (not her floor) to give us the latest medical bulletin. She spoke in her usual dull monotone, fretting as though the Sword of Damocles hovered dangerously above her thin, pale neck.

"Oy, he's *gotta* be okay!" she said; "I don't know what I'd do without him, my poor Harry," those tiny brown eyes darting nervously back and forth, pleading with us to appreciate the gravity of her plight.

We assured her that Harry would be okay, told her not to worry. I wanted to say *he's too ornery to die*, but of course I didn't.

"I've been going every day to visit him—every day!—like a good wife, but I had some things I had to do today, so I haven't gone yet. My friend Alice was gonna pick me up and take me, but…something came up so now she can't." She shook her head sadly, as if to say, 'Oy, what am I gonna do?' "I have to get there; I just *have* to, he expects me. You know? If I don't show up he'll have another stroke—the big one this time. You know? He gets so crazy, my Harry. What am I gonna do?"

Then she just zipped it up and silently stared at me. Just like a Pro, she'd shut up after firing off her close. The silence was thick as the mist in a rainforest, a thousand pounds of pressure per square inch between us. I remember thinking, *So this is what it's like to be on the other end of a close.*

What could I do? What would *you* have done? I bought. Yup, I offered to take her. "I'll come up and get you right after dinner," I promised. "We should be through in about an hour. Okay?"

You'd have thought I'd offered to donate a kidney, the way she went on and on about what a wonderful gesture that was, what a saint I was, God will reward you for your generosity, et cetera, ad nauseam. The Mouse could really pour it on. I'd never heard a better post-close.

About a half-hour later Nicki and I were in the middle of dinner when the doorbell rang. And there, all dressed up and ready to go, purse in hand, stood the Mouse.

I explained that we were still eating dinner.

"Oh…." Those "woe is me" eyes glistening like a poor lost cocker spaniel.

I reminded her I'd said 'about an hour.'

"Oh…." That "poor me, what am I gonna do?" countenance cutting me to the quick, bleeding out every drop of resistance. She finished me off with, "It's just that the visiting hours will be over so soon, you know? I've *gotta* get there! I'm so afraid for my poor suffering Harry…."

I inhaled deeply and sighed. Then I went to get my jacket, umbrella, and car keys. Dinner would have to wait.

I'd been ambushed by a stealthy super-saleswoman; one who wasn't going to take no for an answer. It would have been easier to deny Attila the Hun than the Mouse.

Now this woman no doubt would have told you she couldn't sell to save her life. Most "experts" would have sized up the Mouse and predicted she couldn't sell free rice to the Japanese, and bet their lives on it.

They all would've been dead wrong. Whether or not you approve of her modus operandi, when motivated, the Mouse could get anybody to do her bidding.

She had her methods.

And so do we all.

Jake Terson

My younger son has his own business teaching children how to swim and providing personal training for adults. He's a master at what he does; so much so that the word has gone out all over Chicago's North Shore: if you want your kids to learn how to swim, take them to Jake Terson.

I rarely can sit in a restaurant with Jake, or anywhere else for that matter, without running into some of these parents. I sit and marvel at his interaction with them. They *adore* him! And why not?—they're entrusting their most precious possessions, *their children*, to his care. Not only is he a master of his work, Jake is a master at selling himself to these people. He does it simply by being himself: personable, funny, confident, charming; recalling names, birthdays, and other particulars about their offspring with his phenomenal memory; and always letting them know how much he cares about those kids—and it's the real deal, I assure you. On top of all that, when they watch him with his own two daughters, Jazmine and Jordana, that seals the deal. Jake is one of the best fathers I've ever known. My pride has no boundaries.

Jake is an incredibly effective salesperson, whether he knows it or not.

So are you, and utilizing your instinctive selling acumen to be a fearless top-tier sales professional is a real possibility—I promise you.

3
Are Salespeople Born or Made?

"While it is doubtless true that salesmen, like poets, are born, not made, it is also true that successful salesmen are those who, in most cases, have undergone a severe training in the school of hard knocks."

Farm Journal (October, 1913)

The age-old question "Are salespeople born or made?" has been asked, especially by employers, since the first salesperson made the first call, which probably was before Socrates asked his first question.

The answer is both.

Since we're all salespeople, what faculties does the born salesperson have that others must work their butts off to develop?

Gift of Gab

The born salesperson possesses the gift of gab. He's comfortable talking to anyone at any time. He can be standing behind an attractive woman at the supermarket checkout counter and, out of the clear blue, initiate a conversation with her. He can do this easily as tying his shoelaces.

"You're a Pepsi gal, I see."

She smiles, says, "Actually I buy whatever is on sale."

"Ah, a clever woman—my favorite kind."

Turns out she's single, too; they walk out together and exchange cell numbers.

It's that simple.

This attribute can be developed by anyone bold enough to practice it. As an exercise, for 30 days push yourself to initiate as many "cold-call" conversations as possible with total strangers.

You'll cultivate your gift-of-gab skills and probably meet some interesting people. If you're single, you'll discover it's a fabulous way to meet members of the opposite sex.

Emotional Radar Detector

In addition to the gift of gab, the born salesperson possesses an emotional "radar detector" (see Part IV, Chapter 48, "The Sixth Sense"), which his less fortunate colleagues lack. When he sits across from his prospect, this "radar" *instinctively* reveals how the prospect is reacting emotionally to the presentation—through body language, facial expression, eye contact or lack of eye contact, strength of commitments, and responses to trial closes. This "radar" also works for this lucky individual in social situations, as well as professionally. He can be on a blind date and sense whether or not he's connecting with his companion.

Where does this gift of gab and "radar" come from? Are they innate gifts, or are environmental factors involved? In my opinion, it's a little of both. Psychologists have been debating the heredity/environment question for decades.

For 40 years I sat across from some of the toughest businesspeople your imagination can conjure up, and rarely within the first five minutes did I not sense how the presentation was going. Think of it as something akin to a perceptive poker player reading his opponents.

Can this faculty be assimilated, too? Sure it can: by focusing like a sharp-eyed bald eagle on the prospect's body language, facial expression, eye contact or lack of eye contact, strength of commitments, and responses to trial closes.

As an additional exercise for the next 30 days, when you're engaged in conversation, pay close attention to the first three points listed above. Watch and take note as a whole new dimension of information opens up to you. It won't become instinctive overnight, but given enough time and experience it'll happen. Like anything else in life worth attaining, you must keep at it with the perseverance of a marathon runner.

Musician Turned Salesman

Thirty-eight years ago my kid brother, Harlan, decided to temporarily join me in my business selling advertising. He wanted to make some money—quickly. Harlan is a highly respected blues bass player in Chicago. He's performed all over the world and teaches at The Old Town School of Folk Music. His advertising adventure lasted nine months; once his financial need was sated, he returned to his true vocation—music.

Despite his wicked sense of humor (I've always been Jack Benny to his George Burns—he can make me laugh at will), Harlan is rather laid back, an introvert, the antithesis of most people's image of a creative-intangible salesperson.

I was as determined as a mother bear guarding her cub to turn my brother into a quality salesman. I meticulously taught him the presentation, took him into the field for two months to observe, and painstakingly armed him with the rest of the firepower he needed to succeed. I never put so much of myself into training anyone. Also, our father, Al, a great salesman himself, joined us in the field every Wednesday and spoon-fed Harlan the hot broth of closing sales.

This was family; failure was not an option.

They're never going to enshrine my brother in the Selling Hall of Fame, but he did well enough to meet his financial goal and developed a fairly effective "radar detector" by the time his selling career was over.

Bob Trudeau liked to say, "You can't make a silk purse out of a sow's ear."

He was right and he was wrong.

Harlan was nowhere near a silk purse, but, with all that training and hard work, you would have had a tough time differentiating the "imitation," from the real thing.

If you're a born salesperson, you instinctively know it; if you're not, take heart: what isn't intuitive today soon will be, if you're determined enough to make it happen.

4

Do You Have to Believe in Your Product or Service?

"Personality can open doors,
but only character can keep them open."

Elmer G. Letterman (1897–1982)

Another age-old selling question is, "Do you have to believe in your product or service to be successful?" It depends on your character, your definition of "successful," and your reason for being a salesperson. If you have a conscience and serving the customer/client is paramount, you must believe in what you're selling; if you're in it just to make a living and don't give a hoot whom you exploit, believing in what you sell is not a necessity.

Think of all the con artists who refer to their victims as "marks." Surely they don't believe in their "product" or "service."

Exploitive "Salespeople"

There are "salespeople" who are but a step above the con artist. They're not there to serve people; they're there to milk them. They're not there to provide value, the hallmark of a professional salesperson. Their chutzpah, silver tongues, and power of persuasion churn out positive results—for themselves only; for a while, anyway. These "salespeople" give the selling profession a bad name.

When I began my career in telephone-book-cover advertising, in October 1969, I was part of a five-man crew. Two—we'll call them Keith and Carl—were prime examples of exploitive salespeople. Keith was 36, exceedingly good-looking, a great storyteller and womanizer. He was the top producer in the crew. Carl was 10 years

Keith's junior and absolutely worshiped him; he wanted to be just like his hero. Carl was heavyset, coarse around the edges; Trudeau referred to him as "a diamond in the rough." He showed glimmers of promise but never lived up to it. He was low man on the totem pole.

We met every morning for breakfast before starting work; Trudeau often joined us. It rubbed me the wrong way that Keith and Carl referred to their clients as "mooches"—easy prey. At best, it was disrespectful; at worst, insulting and demeaning.

There isn't one of you who hasn't experienced a Keith or a Carl, which is why, as a society, we're so distrustful of salespeople. Most of us would rather go for a root canal than purchase an automobile.

Do You Believe in Win-Win?

It doesn't have to be this way, and you don't have to be exploitive to be successful. You'll make more money and be a lot happier with yourself if you put the customer's needs and welfare above your own and sell him only what you believe is in his best interest. You can be creative, help him make money where he couldn't visualize the possibility, and be the leader in a win-win relationship, instead of a manipulative parasite.

Treat your role strictly as a fiduciary responsibility and you're on the right path to selling glory. You won't make *every* customer happy: some people you couldn't please if you gave them gold bars, but that doesn't matter, as long as *you* know you're doing right by them, that you're providing real value, that you're a value-based salesperson.

What it comes down to is how you view yourself and others. Do you want to be worthy of respect or don't you care? Do you have a conscience or are you devoid of one? Do you like people or see them as irritants, pains in the derriere? Do you believe in win-win or not?

If it doesn't feel like win-win, something is amiss. As Miss Margaret Sullivan—my grammar school librarian—used to say, "Let your conscience be your guide."

5

The Power and Security of Straight Commission

"There is no security on this earth, there is only opportunity."

General Douglas MacArthur (1889-1964)

Salespeople earn money three ways: salary, salary plus commission, and straight commission. In *Selling Fearlessly*, we're talking mainly straight commission. I never would demean a salary salesperson (straight-commission salespeople have referred to them sarcastically as "order-takers"), but I'd never encourage you to be one. In the selling profession, risk equals reward. If you want big money and unparalleled job security, straight commission is the only way to fly.

Supply and Demand

If you're running a department store and there's an opening in the Men's Department, how many prospective employees do you think will apply for the job at, say, \$15 an hour? Quite a few I'd wager, especially in a high-unemployment job market. I'd also wager that many would do the job satisfactorily for that \$15 an hour. The level of job difficulty is always commensurate with the remuneration offered; it's an employment axiom.

Think you'll find as many candidates dynamic and hungry enough to *create* business out of *nothing*, willing to work for the same \$15 an hour? Hardly, the same axiom is applicable. The personalities and their monetary goals are 180 degrees apart. As Sherlock Holmes would say: "It's elementary."

Job Security

Most salary salespeople need the "security" of a set income. They need to know they're going to get paid regardless of the results produced. Trouble is their "security" too often lasts right up until they're laid off or "let go," which has occurred far more during the Great Recession than any of us thought possible before it began. The irony is that these same people see the straight-commission salesperson *as the one at risk*. After all, for the straight-commission salesperson no results equals no pay—a *terrifying* prospect for salary salespeople. They do not comprehend how much real security they've surrendered for what they erroneously perceive as "security."

The straight-commission salesperson is not interested in guarantees. She knows that accepting any guarantee will cost her dearly, both monetarily *and* in job security. She's an individualist who seeks the maximum income commensurate with what she's willing to expend in effort. She believes in herself; she's willing to toss all her chips into the pot, believing she has the talent to win big. She wants to be paid what she's truly worth, not what someone else *thinks* she's worth. She knows true worth equals true job security. Who's going to fire a top producer making the company a ton of money? Her talent and success are her security.

Even though it was my own company, I paid myself by straight commission plus company profit. I loved the thrill of untold possibilities. How high could I reach? It excited me; it challenged me; more important, it *motivated* me. All the talent in the world will come to nothing if you're not motivated.

Are you motivated, hungry?

Are you ready to bet on yourself to earn your true worth, a worth that soars high in the stratosphere?

A master salesperson always bets on herself.

6

Nothing Happens Until Someone Sells Something

"Nothing happens until something moves."

Albert Einstein (1879-1955)

A salesperson is the engineer of commerce. Until he takes action, *nothing happens*.

If he doesn't sell his advertising on telephone-book-covers, businesses go without customers; artwork, silk-screening, and mail-house venders go without orders; and the homeowner doesn't get the free protective cover she loves.

If the real estate salesperson doesn't sell the house, movers sit idle; appliance, hardware, lawn equipment, and furniture stores are ghost towns; and the teenage boy across the street doesn't get a job mowing the lawn.

If the life insurance salesperson doesn't sell the policy, an entire home-office support system sits around twiddling their thumbs; and somewhere a widow in her mid-30s, with three young children to support, does not have the means to keep a roof over their heads and food on the table.

Ripples of idleness and destruction spreading business-killing misery across the pond.

Nothing happens until someone sells something.

It Begins with You

You are absolutely vital; the lifeblood of the economy is in your hands. Doesn't that amaze you? It did me. It made me realize how meaningful my work was. I was doing something important, my profession was important, the business world stood dormant until millions of my colleagues and I took action. We all want to be important—it's exhilarating, heart-swelling to your mental attitude. We'll talk about mental attitude in Part II.

Salesman for the Gods

Used-car salespeople are maligned as often as mosquitoes breed. If a newspaper columnist wants to express contempt for the group she's writing about, she'll likely compare them to used-car salespeople. I recall a sour photograph of Richard Nixon, with the caption, "Would you buy a used car from this man?"

My first car was a *very* used '57 Chevy; I was 19. I'll never forget the genial man who sold it to me. I don't recall his name, but he was in his mid-to-late 50s, about six-foot-three, 280—a big guy. He had a cheerful smile, an infectious laugh, and a comforting baritone voice, and he knew cars like Einstein knew physics. Most important, though, the man loved selling cars. He could have rushed me to get to another customer worth a lot more commission than that $450 beat-up old Chevy, but he took his sweet time with me, relishing helping a nervous young man buy his first automobile. He patiently answered every question like a father teaching his son how to change the oil and filter, and oh how I wish I could thank him again and tell him what his professionalism and kindness meant to me.

It was *Everything*, that's how important that first car was to me.

Yes, I got lucky. Not all used-car salespeople are as professional and caring; but on *that* day, at *that* dealership, I met a used-car salesman who deserved to stand with the gods.

He made something happen that truly enriched my life.

Do me a favor: keep him in mind the next time you observe someone contemptuous of used-car salespeople.

7

Success Is a By-product of Preparation and Execution

"It's not the will to win that matters—everyone has that. It's the will to prepare to win that matters."

Paul "Bear" Bryant (1919-1983)

I often fantasize about how I would perform in other professions. As a college basketball coach, for example, what I'd say to my team before the first practice, so they'd fully comprehend my philosophy about winning and losing juxtaposed to preparation and execution. A team should know what their coach expects of them.

Question and Answer Session

My players are seated in a semicircle at the side of the court as I address them. This is the most crucial moment of the season, because if they don't "get it," they'll never be successful.

"Anyone here like to lose?"

A few snickers but no one responds, because, after all, it's a rhetorical question—no one likes to lose.

"Okay, let me ask you this: What do you think is more important, winning or losing, or how well you prepare and execute?"

Silence.

My eyes bore into them; I wait for someone to take a risk and speak out. Finally, one cautiously raises his hand, says, "Vince Lombardi said, 'Winning isn't everything, it's the only thing'."

As it turns out, the young man didn't take much of a risk: *he* didn't say it, Vince Lombardi did, and who's going to argue with the great Vince Lombardi? He doesn't realize it, but he's invoked third-party affirmation, which is a powerful tool when handling objections. (We'll get to third-party affirmation in Part IV, Chapter 50, "Overcoming Objections.")

"Do you all agree?"

Nodding of heads, a few mumbled, "Yeah"s, and then more silence.

I don't know if it would go that way, but it's my imagination so…

Motivating Speech

"I want you all to listen carefully; I'm about to tell you the most important thing you'll ever need to know about winning basketball games, or for that matter, anything else in life. Yeah, we're here to win; winning is important. Winning is like a succulent strawberry in season; losing is an agonizing trip to hell in a hand basket. If we don't win, I'll be vilified in the press right up to the point they hang me in effigy and fire me. You'll be vilified in the press and become the loneliest outcasts on campus, and we'll all rationalize our debacle for the rest of our laughingstock lives.

"Now, that said, I'll tell you that I don't give a damn about winning or losing. I simply want you to prepare to the Nth degree and then, when it's time to play, execute as close to perfection as you possibly can.

"If given a choice between winning while playing a sloppy, poorly executed game, or losing while executing to perfection, I'll take the latter any day of the week, because winning is simply a by-product of preparation and execution. You *win* by preparation and execution; you *lose* by being cavalier about preparation and execution. Just ask Michael Jordan what he thinks of Allen Iverson's rant about practice. Or Larry Bird, who always showed up early to shoot at least two hours of practice shots.

"If you fully prepare, as though your lives depend on it, and leave *everything* you've got on that court, in a way we both can be proud of, I'll never utter a critical word because we lost the game—I don't care if it's the NCAA National Championship Game.

"Do I make myself clear?"

What You Must Do

You must prepare to the utmost degree just like the athlete. You must know your presentation like your ABCs. You must know every objection and have a rebuttal for each one, a rebuttal you'll confidently execute to neutralize the objection. Anything less and I promise you, you'll fail. I trained many a salesperson, and rarely did one succeed who didn't *fully* prepare before going into the field. Executing effectively when you're ill-prepared is like trying to speak Swahili in Russia—you'll look like a fool.

Memorize this: Success is a *by-product* of preparation and execution. Emulate Larry Bird's work ethic and you, too, will be a champion.

8

They'll Buy if They Like You

"If you make it plain you like people, it's hard for them to resist liking you back."

Lois McMaster Bujold (*Diplomatic Immunity*, 2002)

Last year, Nicki and I checked out the iPad® and iPhone® at the Apple Store in the Woodfield Mall. Bewitching toys, but I was so much more *WOWED* by the young salesman, Andy Pasek, who showed us how to "play" with them. Andy had a tall, athletic build, intelligent brown eyes, and a beaming smile that could light up a coal mine.

He approached me while Nicki was trying out the iPad; I stood right next to her. He enthusiastically thrust out his hand and in a booming, confident voice said, "Can I show you something?"

I Liked Him

My initial reaction was no, we hadn't come to buy anything, but that lasted all of three seconds because—you know what?—I *wanted* this "kid" (Andy's in his mid-20s, that's a kid to me) to show me something because I instantly *liked* him. There was just something bright, energetic, *fearless*, and ineffably delightful about him. Initially he asked a series of probing questions: what kind of computers and cell phones did we have? How and for what purposes did we use them? What were our most passionate interests? I mentioned the book I was writing, as an example. Once he was armed with the specifics he needed, he demonstrated the mind-boggling functions of the iPad and iPhone, with all the technological dexterity his generation commands. Admiration for Andy's selling mastery flooded over me like a tsunami. So impressed was I that I'll offer this highly subjective opinion: whatever they're paying him—a salary or an hourly wage—it isn't enough. Not by a long shot.

Andy Pasek, because I liked him so much, was able to take me in 15 short minutes from "I just use a cell phone to make phone calls" to "I absolutely have to have one of those gadgets"—a mega-watt transition that astounded me.

When a Prospect Likes You

When a prospect likes you, sales resistance disappears like a burnt-off morning fog. We dropped by to kill some time, check out the toys we'd heard so much about. We had not a scintilla of desire to *buy* anything, but after Andy's dynamic iPhone presentation, we both had to have one, and recently we each purchased an iPad, too. We're having a ton of fun with both products. Thanks, Andy!

If your prospects like you, they'll have the same strong desire to buy from you, especially if you dazzle them with your presentation à la Andy Pasek.

So, are you likeable? Do you present yourself in a likeable manner? It's something you can't fake—you either are or you're not; you either do or you don't. Keep in mind: we're talking about being *likeable*, not the salesperson's need to be liked; the former is a strength, the latter a weakness.

Ask yourself, what causes *you* to like a salesperson? Conversely, what turns you off quicker than the blink of an eye? Here's a short list of what made Andy so likeable to me: He was genuine, personable, enthusiastic, friendly, funny, professional, and *knowledgeable*, and he was so eager to show us his incredible wares, then excitedly demonstrated those wares, *in relation to our interests*, like a joyful child playing with his new train set on Christmas morning; and because he was having *so much fun* doing it, so did we.

Other than price, how much they like you is the foremost reason why customers will, or won't, buy from you. You may have *exactly* what they want; they may have driven 200 miles to buy it; everything from price to financing to delivery is perfect; but if they don't like you, they'll take a hike and buy it someplace else, from a salesperson they do like.

Likeability—ignore it and you'll push the envelope of providence.

9
The Triangle

"The triangle is a foundation to an offense."
Bill Cartwright (Chicago Bulls center)

I was taught the Triangle by Bob Trudeau while undergoing sales training. Where Trudeau learned about it I know not, but he believed in it passionately, and 43 years later I can say it meant more to my success as a salesman than any other tidbit of information.

We all tell a story in our own imitable style, and if today Trudeau listened to *my* rendition of the Triangle, no doubt he'd hear an altered version; but I hope he'd be pleased that I've passed on the Triangle to hundreds of people, in speeches, sales seminars, and airplanes I flew to and from work. I'd reach for pen and paper, draw a triangle, label each side, and tell my story.

The triangle is a sturdy geometric figure, if all three sides are solidly connected; otherwise all you have is a wobbly structure, which eventually will crumble into a pile of naught.

Mental Attitude

The first side is Mental Attitude. You must possess a positive mental attitude made out of titanium. *Anyone* can be up when she's winning, when everything is running like a well-oiled machine and success is the norm; show me a salesperson who is alert and grinning, enthusiastic, ready to forge ahead and make that next call after she's had her teeth kicked in for a month and a half and I'll show you a Champion.

Work Habits

The second side is Work Habits. I don't care how talented you are, or if you possess the selling acumen of Brian Tracy, Dr. Tony

Alessandra, and Tom Hopkins combined, no one defiles Mother Law of Averages and gets away with it long term. You must always do the work. For a salesperson, that means making the calls, giving presentations. There is no compromise. Given the choice of a salesperson who gives six presentations a week and closes 60%, or one who gives ten presentations a week and closes 40%, I'll take the latter on any day that ends in "Y."

Salesmanship

Side three is Salesmanship. If *anyone* knows your business better than you, best take a hard look in the mirror and ask why. If *anyone* knows the intricacies of selling techniques better than you, time to challenge yourself again. There are no excuses, no alibis. It's your business, your choice of making a living; you must know every aspect of your business—backwards, forwards, and sideways. You must know selling techniques down to the subtlest detail.

Lever and Fulcrum

The Triangle is the lever and fulcrum of successful selling. Archimedes said, "Give me a lever long enough, and a fulcrum on which to place it, and I shall move the world." If your Triangle is sturdy enough, *you'll* move the world. Everything you need to know, all the answers, fall under the purview of one of its three sides. In Part II we'll discuss Mental Attitude; Part III, Work Habits; and Part IV, Salesmanship.

You can count on the Triangle; it'll never let you down. You also can count on utter failure unless *all three sides* are functioning in a robust manner.

It's sort of like the lyrics from "Love and Marriage": "you can't have one without the other[s]"

Draw a large triangle and label its three sides. Frame it and place it where you'll see it every day.

Are you ready to move the world?

PART II

MENTAL ATTITUDE

10
Motivation

"People who are unable to motivate themselves must be content with mediocrity, no matter how impressive their other talents."
Andrew Carnegie (1835-1919)

The first element of mental attitude is motivation; it propels us towards desire and belief, and compels us to take action, no matter how long the odds. The eternal question is "Why are some driven and others not?" If you're not hungry, obsessed to succeed, you lack the fuel to ignite your rocket to the stars; you may blow a lot of smoke, but you're not going anywhere.

I've known salespeople more educated and a lot smarter than me, but alas, all too often their selling careers came to naught because they lacked the spark plug of motivation. Perhaps they'd have been better off attending the School of Hard Knocks.

Personal History

Allow me to share some personal history, which pinpoints what motivated me to become a lifelong achiever: money often was a thorny issue for my family. It was feast or famine, with *way* too much time on the famine side of the ledger. Its apex hit when I was 19, when my father left us. I didn't know where he was for three long years. After foreclosure proceedings, the modest townhouse we lived in was repossessed; that was 1963. Today I weep for the wretched souls who have been thrown out of their homes, especially the children.

My mother went to work in a clothing store for $60 a week; I got a job at Bankers Life and Casualty Company for $90 a week and went to DePaul University nights and Saturdays. We moved into a dinky three-and-a-half-room third-floor apartment—my mother, grandmother, brother (he was 12), and me; I slept in a hallway. We probably qualified for welfare but were too proud to ask for it. I was an angry young man who *vowed* I'd live my life much differently. I was going to be successful and live well, so too my family; poverty was about as much fun as jumping out of an airplane without a parachute, far more frightening than any prospect. It robbed you of your dignity, humiliated you, poisoned your self-esteem, and left you scarred for life. Those bitter memories stalked me, drove me, and explain why I never take anything for granted, why I sold fearlessly. There is poverty and there is success, and success is a hell of a lot more fun.

So there you have it—the fuel for my fire.

Michael Jordan

I'm a Chicago guy, which makes me a Bulls fan, and you can't be a Bulls fan without revering the basketball prowess of Michael Jordan. What strikes me most about Jordan is how he motivated himself. The slightest perceived insult, disparaging quote to the press, or challenge to his pecking order amongst the greats of the game—Robertson, Russell, Bird, Jabbar, Chamberlain, Baylor, Magic Johnson—he'd absorb these aspersions like a sponge and mentally challenge himself to thrash, humiliate, destroy you. The man's fiery will to be the best and defeat all pretenders is legendary; he instilled fear just by stepping onto the court. Some say he's still driven to show up his freshman-year high school coach for cutting him from the team.

Whatever works, right?

You must know yourself through and through, understand what makes you tick; then dig deep within yourself to find some motivational kindling to ignite your hunger, spur you on towards desire and belief.

Once you're motivated, you're ready to pursue success.

If you're *not* motivated, if you don't want it badly enough, if you're more afraid of the prospect than you are of failure, you and your family have my deepest sympathies, because you're not going to succeed even if God Himself is holding your hand.

11
Desire

"Desire. That's the one secret of every man's career. Not education. Not being born with hidden talents. Desire."

Bobby Unser

I longed to be a salesman because, as a child, I'd gobbled up all my father's amazing tales and hungered to compete in the same arena. My desire was amplified after he left us. I was infuriated with him and driven to outshine him at his own game. Even negative emotions like anger and revenge can create desire. I don't recommend them, but I clearly understand the passion they generate.

My father grew considerably later in life, and in many ways he became a man to be admired. He proved worthy of forgiveness, which was more than enough for me. I loved him dearly. He passed away on January 21, 2010, and I miss him terribly. He would have been thrilled to know I was writing this book.

If you lack the desire to be a salesperson, you'll be like a mountain climber attempting Mount Everest without any protective clothing or gear: you won't get very far. If the desire *is* there, you must nurture it.

Visualization

You must focus on your desire until you're completely obsessed by it. You must visualize yourself *already* selling like a master, living the rewarding life of a master salesperson. The more detailed you make it, the more powerful it'll be; try to get all five senses involved. The Reverend Dr. Norman Vincent Peale said, "Formulate and stamp indelibly on your mind a mental picture of yourself as succeeding. Hold this picture tenaciously and never permit it to fade. Your mind will seek to develop this picture!"

The importance of your vision can't be overstated. What you're doing is sending a clear-cut order, via autosuggestion, to the computer-command-center of your being, your subconscious mind. You also must verbally affirm the order at least ten times a day so your subconscious will know you're serious about your desire; anything less than full cooperation will not be tolerated:

> My desire is already mine;
> it's waiting for me to take charge of it;
> so henceforth you are to guide and direct me,
> with no equivocation whatsoever,
> until my desire is realized.

Blend with Love

Is there a significant other in your life? Are you in love? Do you want it for both of you? Here's a little secret: blend desire with love and you'll create an order to your subconscious so powerful the gods will kneel at your feet. Nicki and I are well into our fourth decade together, my love for her spurring me on to ever-greater heights.

Add Inspiring Music

Season your desire/love order with inspiring music and, well, the goose bumps will make you weep. Look up the lyrics to "I Don Quixote" from *Man of La Mancha,* memorize them, and you'll be on your way to great glory.

I love inspiring music; it heightens desire to a fever pitch. I can listen to "Chariots of Fire" and suddenly I'm Eric Liddle running the 400 meters in the 1924 Olympics, I'm unstoppable.

Or the late Whitney Houston's rendition of "One Moment in Time." I defy you to listen to the lyrics of that song without chills running up and down your spine. Your dreams, too, will be a heart-beat away.

Inspiring Films

Movies, too, can be awe-inspiring. One of my favorite films is *Rudy*. If you haven't seen it, rent it and you'll be ready to charge a windmill à la Don Quixote. It's the story of an ordinary man with an extraordinary desire. I've seen it a dozen times and never fail to weep as his teammates hoist Rudy Ruettiger atop their shoulders and triumphantly carry him off the Notre Dame field, the roar of the crowd deafening.

Everything Ruettiger battled through to fulfill his desire to (1) become a Notre Dame student, (2) become a member of the Notre Dame football team, and (3) finally get into a Fighting Irish home game at South Bend, in front of his father and brother, makes "The Mound Road Story" seem like a series of minor inconveniences.

Rudy had a desire as big as Atlas's to hoist the earth onto his shoulders, *and he was not going to be denied*!

How About You?

Dr. Robert H. Schuller said, "You can often measure a person by the size of his dream." Is the power of your desire comparable to Rudy Ruettiger's? Do you want to be a master salesperson as much as Rudy wanted to be a Notre Dame student and football player?

I can imagine the kind of master salesperson Rudy would have been; are you willing to run the gauntlet like he did, to become that master salesperson?

Remember, your dream is *already* yours, just waiting for you to claim it.

How incredible that's going to be for you.

Never stop dreaming your dream.

12
Belief

"They can conquer who believe they can."
Virgil (70 BC-19 BC)

The majority of us vastly underestimate our power; it's human nature 101. Believing in ourselves doesn't come easy. My father used to say, "There's no substitute for experience." But if you're a rookie who hasn't made his first call yet, how do you come up with enough confidence to tell yourself, "Yeah, I can do this thing," and believe it? And you *must* believe it. Napoleon Hill, in his classic, *Think and Grow Rich*, said, "Whatever the mind of man can conceive and *believe* [my emphasis], it can achieve."

Leap of Faith

You do it by making a leap of faith, the same way religious people do, and the only possible way to make that leap of faith is to win over your subconscious mind by repeating at least ten times a day, via auto-suggestion, the following determination mantra (growl it if it makes you more determined):

> I can do this;
> I know I can do this;
> I'm going to do this;
> there isn't anyone or anything
> that's going to stop me from doing this—
> period!

It may take some time, but eventually your subconscious will be convinced and you'll truly believe, Faith will be yours. It matters not how long the odds, how "impossible" the quest, how scared you are, or if you start out faking it; once your subconscious has been convinced and you believe in yourself, you're 80% there. Most people will tell you that seeing is believing; in truth, believing is seeing. A cheap trick or a mind skill? Does it matter, as long as it works? Personally, I see it as a mind skill.

A Young Boy Dreams

If becoming a master salesperson seems like a stretch-and-a-half to you, try *this* dream on for size:

In the early 1970s a young boy dreams about being a great athlete; if you're male, with two good arms and legs, and haven't experienced this fantasy at least 10,000 times before you're 18, you're not human.

But what if you only have *one* arm and a stump, what then? Could you still seriously dream of being an athlete and truly believe it's possible?

This kid did.

His name is Jim Abbott and he never stopped believing, or allowed anyone or anything to stand in the way of his dream. He had faith in himself.

Abbott was born September 19, 1967, in Flint, Michigan. He was born without a right hand, just the stump I mentioned. Despite his great physical handicap, he indeed became an athlete. He was the starting quarterback of his high school football team; they made it to the finals of the Michigan state championship. His true sport, though, was baseball. Unbelievably, he chose to be a pitcher. He wore a right-handed glove over the stump, then quickly switched the glove to his left hand after completing his pitching motion so he'd be ready to field his position. He'd remove the glove in a flash and make the throw with his left hand. He started perfecting this amazing technique at the ripe old age of 4.

Abbott went to the University of Michigan on a baseball scholarship. He led the Wolverines to the Big Ten title in his freshman and junior years. He won the Golden Spikes Award, given to the outstanding college baseball player in the United States. He was a member of the 1987 American team at the Pan American Games and won the U.S. Federation's Golden Spikes Award—best amateur player in the country. In 1988 he led his country to the Gold Medal in the Olympic Games. He also won the Sullivan Award that year—best amateur athlete in the United States. The following year he joined the California Angels, beginning a 12-year major-league career. In 1991 Abbott won 18 games for the Angels, with an ERA of 2.89, and finished third in the running for the American League Cy Young Award.

On September 4, 1993, in the hallowed halls of the original Yankee Stadium, Abbott hurled a no-hitter against the Cleveland Indians.

I never met Jim Abbott, but as you can gather, I'm in awe of him. To have that kind of faith in yourself, to be that blind to your—you should pardon the expression—"handicap," seems, well, a billion miles beyond "an ordinary man doing an extraordinary thing." Line up 50,000 men and women; how many do you think would possess that kind of space-age-alloy mental attitude?

Good luck.

Your selling gauntlet is mere child's play, by comparison.

Even after you become an old Pro, belief in yourself, true confidence that you can perform successfully in a specific arena of life, can come and go as capriciously as the weather in Chicago (around here we've been known to "brag": "If you don't like the weather, wait a minute").

Just Ask Brad Lidge

Brad Lidge also is a major league pitcher, a relief pitcher, one of the best closers in the game. In 2005 he was the closer for the Houston Astros, and because of his considerable success that year, he was a major reason the Astros made the playoffs and wound up facing the St. Louis Cardinals in the best-of-seven National League Championship Series.

In game five of the NLCS, at Houston's Minute Maid Park, in the ninth inning, Lidge was brought in—his team ahead three to one in games, with a score of 4 to 2 in game five—to mop up the Cardinals and put the Astros into the World Series. He got the first two batters out, but then gave up a two-strike single (that's right, he was *one* strike away from Valhalla) to David Eckstein and walked Jim Edmonds.

Oops, now he had to face Albert Pujols, arguably the best hitter in baseball. All Pujols did was *CRUSH* a dramatic line-drive that *SLAMMED* high off the wall behind the left-field Crawford Boxes—home run. I've never seen a baseball leave the field quicker than that one did; if there hadn't been a wall there, it might still be going. The TV camera took a shot of the Astros' dugout, and Andy Petitte, eyes wide as quarters, mouthed the words, "Oh my God!"

According to an e-mail making the rounds, on the plane ride back to St. Louis, the Astros' catcher, Brad Ausmus, went up to Lidge and said, "You know that home run Pujols hit?—it just flew by." The Astros had lost game five, but fortunately came back to win game six and advance to their first World Series.

Lidge didn't get off so easy. Oh, he played in the 2005 World Series, but he sure wasn't the same effective pitcher in that series or *the next two seasons*. It got so bad the Astros traded him after 2007 to the Phillies.

One home run, that's all it took to turn "Lights-out-Lidge" into "Blank-Cartridge-Brad" for tens of millions of baseball fans.

The conventional wisdom says it was mental.

Gee, you think?

Here's the knock-me-down-with-a-feather punch line to the Lidge saga. In 2008 he was his old self again *and then some*. He led the Phillies to the National League Pennant, saving 41 out of 41 games, unheard of *perfection*, and was named MLB Comeback Player of the Year.

Hero to Goat to Hero.

We're All Tested

Confidence can be stripped away in the blink of an eye and, as in Lidge's case, it can take a chunk of your life to get it back. Some are doomed never to get it back. Somewhere along the way, you *will* be tested, it goes with the territory. Every salesperson—even a master salesperson—will face a bleak, hopeless slump when everything goes wrong and doubt renders him numb as a paralyzing stroke.

Henry Ford once said, "If you think you can do a thing or if you think you can't do a thing, you're right."

Shoe Salesperson Story

There's a famous story of a shoe salesperson who was sent to open up a new territory on a Pacific island. After a week, he sent a telegram to the home office: "Whoever came up with this idea ought to be shot at dawn—they don't wear shoes here." The company sent a second salesperson to the same island. She sent a telegram, too; it read, "Whoever came up with this idea is a genius—they all need shoes."

If you think you can, if you believe, it shall be yours.

13
The Subconscious Mind

"Whatever we plant in our subconscious mind and nourish with repetition and emotion will one day become a reality."
Earl Nightingale (1921-1989)

As previously stated in Chapter 11, "Desire," the subconscious mind is the computer-command-center of your being, the subterranean regulator of your physical, mental, and emotional functioning. Think of it as a mainframe computer regulating the air-conditioning, heating, lighting, elevators, et cetera, in a skyscraper; you can't see it, but it's there running things.

It's in Charge

Information is fed to your subconscious mind by way of the five senses—seeing, hearing, smelling, touching, tasting; your thoughts and emotions; and external sources. The conscious mind is what you're aware of, what René Descartes meant when he said, "I think, therefore I am"; but your subconscious has the real power, is in charge. You can will your conscious mind all you want, but if the subconscious rebels or sees it differently, because of the data *you've* fed it, it will win out.

Writer's block is an example of this principle in action: the blocked writer consciously desires to write, demands it of herself, but is unable to take action because her subconscious won't allow it. Consciously she tells herself she can succeed, but subconsciously she really doesn't believe it, so her subconscious shuts her down, "protects" her from what she's fearful of or doesn't want to face. Ironically, she may be angry with herself, berate herself over her "procrastination" and "laziness." It's nothing of the kind.

A Hypnotist's "Suggestions"

In December 2009 Nicki and I took a 10-day Caribbean cruise. One evening a hypnotist put on a hilarious show. Amongst the 15 or so subjects on stage was a young man who was told his derriere would be on fire every time he heard "and it burns, burns, burns…that ring of fire, that ring of fire"; he also was told he'd have to bounce along on his buttocks like a toddler to cool off his flaming behind. Each time the music played he'd leap out of his chair, ferociously rub his bottom, plop down to the floor, and bounce across the stage, his agonized countenance causing uproarious laughter.

At the end of the show, the hypnotist gave all his subjects a post-hypnotic suggestion: on hearing the trigger word, they "saw" everyone in the audience nude, including family and friends. Their mortified expressions and contortions to cover their eyes or look away were sidesplitting. I would not have been surprised if some in the audience wet their pants laughing.

What was going on here?

What happens to a hypnotized subject?

The subconscious is taken over by the hypnotist's "suggestions." What the subject actually sees, hears, smells, touches, and tastes is powerless to overrule the "truth" of the hypnotist's suggestions. Such is the power of the subconscious.

Learning a New Skill

When you first learn to drive, the conscious mind directs your actions. You feel anxious because you lack experience—it's all so new to you. After a while, though, the subconscious takes over and it becomes second nature, rote—you no longer think about driving. You're on autopilot, it's being done for you; you think about other things, listen to music, imagine the Cubs winning the World Series.

Breathing and Heartbeat

Do you normally pay attention to your breathing or heartbeat? No, they're monitored and controlled by your subconscious, not your conscious mind. On the rare occasions you *do* take notice of your breathing or heartbeat, you become uncomfortable. If this awareness were the norm instead of occasional, you'd be unable to function productively.

Master Problem Solver

The subconscious is the master problem solver, not the conscious mind you pose the problem to. Have you ever gone blank about a name or date? At my age we call that a "senior moment." You've known it for years, if not decades—but suddenly it's gone, poof. You wrack your brain, but it just won't serve up the answer; the next morning while you're brushing your teeth, *bingo*, it pops into your consciousness like a long-lost relative and you wonder how you ever "lost" it. It was there all the time, of course, deep in your subconscious. Philosophers and inventors advise sleeping on a problem because the subconscious performs best while the conscious mind is asleep, delivering the solution during the night or in the morning. Thomas Edison advocated sleeping on a problem.

Garbage in, Garbage Out

The subconscious mind never shuts down; it's constantly sorting, measuring, interpreting, and analyzing the data you feed it, without a shred of bias. Feed it positive thoughts and emotions and it will respond with positive support; feed it negative thoughts and emotions and it will respond negatively. Think of the computer expression "garbage in, garbage out." Be fearful and fear is what you'll get back; be desirous and believing and it will find ways to make it happen for you.

Standing Guard

This is why it's so vital for a salesperson to remain positive, never to wallow in the depths of negativity by feeling sorry for yourself, doubting yourself, blowing a temporary setback completely out of proportion: "I haven't sold a thing in a week and a half; oh woe is me; I probably won't sell anything today, either; in fact, I probably won't sell a damn thing ever again; I might as well quit now."

If you think this soliloquy is farfetched, let me assure you it happens all the time. Too many salespeople do not vigilantly stand guard over their thoughts and emotions. They send out vibrations of fear, doubt, and worry; instead of desire, belief, and determination. They put garbage in, so they get garbage out, unwittingly sabotaging themselves.

You must supply your subconscious with the healthy thoughts and emotions it needs to provide the positive support you'll *continuously* require to succeed. Indulge in negative thinking and emoting and you'll be your own worst enemy. Salespeople who go down for the count usually do so because they self-destructed via negative subconscious programming.

Don't let that happen to you; jealously guard your thoughts and emotions.

"For as he thinketh in his heart, so is he."—Proverbs 23:7.

14
Gratitude

"He is a wise man who does not grieve for the things which he has not, but rejoices for those which he has."
Epictetus (55 AD-135 AD)

I believe the optimum state of mind to accomplish any achievement is gratitude. It doesn't matter what your status is, what you have or don't have, there is *always* something to be grateful for. George Burns, in his mid-90s, said, "Let's face it, at my age, I'm very pleased to be anywhere." For a salesperson, what's significant about gratitude is that it's impossible to feel discouraged or sorry for yourself if you're feeling grateful.

Do you have a spouse you love and who loves you? There are widows and widowers out there who ache for their lost loves; I know a few, they're friends of mine. Do you have children? Are they healthy? Think of the millions of depressed women whose wombs are barren; or the grief-stricken parents of a critically ill child, who desperately go from the ICU to light a candle at church. Are you healthy? My grandmother, born in 1888 on a farm outside of Minsk, used to say, "If you don't have your health, you have nothing." Smart woman, my grandmother. Do you have adequate shelter? The homeless do not. Do you have enough to eat? The hungry do not. Were you educated? The illiterate were not.

The things to be grateful for are endless, are they not?

Gift of Life

Isn't it simply a miracle that you and I are alive on this earth, with limitless opportunities to live life to its fullest? Just to have known love was worth the price of admission. It makes me want to get down on my knees and give thanks to the Powers That Be for every day I've been blessed with, for all the wonderful people I've been blessed with. When I'm told to have a nice day, my standard response is "I woke up this morning; it's already a nice day." How about you? Do you appreciate all your blessings or just take them for granted?

Have you ever heard about the man who complained about not having shoes, until he saw someone in a wheelchair without feet?

Gratitude List

Here's an exercise for you: create a gratitude list; write down everything you're grateful for. You may stop at a hundred, but go to a thousand if you like. At the top of my own gratitude list are the health of my wife, three children, and three grandchildren. I once made a promise to never take their health for granted. I made that promise on a Saturday morning in February 1997, in the CAT-scan waiting room at Lutheran General Hospital.

Kidney Cancer

On a Sunday evening six days earlier, I had deplaned in Atlanta, gone to the bathroom and was shocked out of my wits to see blood in my urine. It happened six more times before I headed home Thursday. I have no excuse for not listening to my wife and immediately going home; not one of my more prudent decisions.

Nicki had set up an appointment with the urologist for Friday, but I went directly from O'Hare Field after my plane landed. The doctor examined me, said there were a number of possibilities, and then sent me to the hospital for an IVP X ray. When I was done with the X ray and about to leave, the technician told me the urologist was on the telephone.

"I'm sorry to have to tell you this," he said, "but I'm afraid I've got bad news—it's kidney cancer, not much doubt about it."

He suggested I return to his office so a surgery date could be set forthwith.

Kidney cancer—it sounded so ominous; I contemplated my mortality.

"Do not ask for whom the bell tolls," Hemingway wrote, "the bell tolls for thee."

CAT Scan

There was little doubt about the diagnosis, but the urologist wanted a CAT scan to be 100% sure. So that's how I wound up in the CAT-scan waiting room early Saturday morning. Nicki and I were alone except for a young couple and their two-and-a-half-year-old daughter—a real cutie. They sat directly across from us.

Nicki nervously explained why we were there; the little girl's mother explained why *they* were there: their daughter had developed a rare cancer when she was six months old, and periodic CAT scans had become part of their routine.

Six months old! *A baby*, *for God's sake*! I fought back the tears—for both of us, but especially that beautiful child and her beleaguered parents. I ached for them.

I tried to imagine what it must have been like for the mother and father to cope with such an ordeal—hell, *still* were coping with it. How did they manage it? A baby whom you couldn't communicate with, explain things to; how could they watch her suffer so without going stark-raving mad? I couldn't do it, I thought. I couldn't possibly deal with something so devastating. Surely I'd collapse and die.

Surge of Gratitude

I felt a surge of gratitude that *I* had the kidney cancer, not one of my kids. I took that CAT scan feeling like Lou Gehrig—"the luckiest man on the face of the earth."

There is *always* something to be grateful for.

It's impossible to feel discouraged or sorry for yourself if you're feeling grateful.

Smell the Roses

There's magic all around you; take notice of it, never take it for granted.

Smell the roses!

Emerson said it so well:

For each new morning with its light,
For rest and shelter of the night,
For health and food, for love and friends,
For everything Thy goodness sends.

Be grateful and inevitably you'll have a lot more to be grateful for.

The salesperson who has a heart full of gratitude sells a lot more than the one who doesn't.

15
Commitment

"Losers make promises they often break.
Winners make commitments they always keep."
Denis Waitley

It's time to make a commitment. "I'm going to give it a shot" is not a commitment. "I'm going to stick with it as long as I can" is not a commitment. A commitment is as irrevocable as enlisting in the French Foreign Legion; it's hard as a diamond, inflexible as a block of steel. It's an ironclad vow, a sworn pledge, to yourself and your Creator, that the *only* thing that will keep you from realizing your desire to become a master salesperson is death itself. *Nothing else* will stop you, because you'll *never* quit. In the immortal words of Sir Winston Churchill: "Never give in, never, never, never, never—in nothing, great or small, large or petty—never give in."

The worst mistake you'll ever make in life is giving up.

Derek Anthony Redmond

In the 1992 Olympic Games in Barcelona, 27-year-old British runner Derek Anthony Redmond ran the 400 meters. He'd posted the fastest time in the first round and won his quarterfinal heat. In his semifinal heat, in the back straight, about 250 meters from the finish line, he pulled a hamstring and fell to the ground in agony. Stretcher bearers rushed to his aid, but Redmond wasn't having any of that, no thank you. He struggled to his feet and limped along the track, a portrait of courageous heartache. Sixty-five-thousand people cheered him on. They cheered even louder when his father, Jim Redmond, broke through security and ran onto the track to aid his son. Together they inched their way around the track until just before the finish line; then Jim Redmond let go and watched his son hobble across the finish line to a thunderous standing ovation. Despite being disqualified, Redmond became an Olympic hero that day. According to Olympic record books, he never finished the race, but to world public opinion, he finished heroically.

The man was committed—not even a pulled hamstring could stop him from crossing that finish line, an inspiration to the world.

Betty Anne Waters

In 1982, Kenny Waters of Ayer, Massachusetts, was charged with murdering a neighbor and sentenced to life without parole. His sister, Betty Anne Waters, an 11th-grade dropout, loved her brother and never stopped believing he was innocent. She made a lifelong commitment to Kenny that she would prove his innocence and free him from the Massachusetts state prison. To do that, she knew she had to become a lawyer; a seemingly impossible task. First she got her GED; then an associate's degree at the Community College of Rhode Island; next a master's in education at Rhode Island College; and finally the law degree at Roger Williams University Law School. It took Waters 13 years to get that law degree. It cost her a marriage and custody of her two sons. With the help of attorney Barry Scheck of the Innocence Project, and DNA evidence that Waters refused to believe had been destroyed, she finally prevailed and freed her brother 18 years after he'd been incarcerated.

"Every day ordinary people do extraordinary things," Bob Richards said. He might have added, "Especially if they've made an extraordinary commitment."

The Biggest Loser

Nicki is a huge fan of reality TV. One of her favorites is *The Biggest Loser*—obese men and women struggling mightily to competitively shed their excess poundage. I watched a number of episodes in 2010, and the winner, Michael Ventrella, became a hero of mine.

Ventrella weighed a whopping 526 pounds going in; he was the heaviest contestant ever to compete on the show. Initially he could hardly move. Week after week Ventrella and his compatriots, to the screaming in-your-face exhortations of *The Biggest Loser* staff, exercised until they collapsed. Never have I seen human beings exert themselves to such all-out physical and mental exhaustion. Near the end of the season the final four contestants ran a *marathon*.

At his final weigh-in, victorious Ventrella weighed a svelte 262 pounds, having lost 50.19% of his body weight, and was the winner of the $250,000 prize. The before-and-after camera shots left me astonished and brought tears to my eyes. Ventrella said, "I knew going onto that ranch that I needed to save my life."

The man made a commitment to *save his life*!

Your Commitment

Is your commitment any less than Michael Ventrella's? Maybe your life isn't at stake, but the *quality* of your life is, the quality of your family's life is. What does that mean to you? Does it mean enough to make a Michael Ventrella commitment? A Derek Anthony Redmond commitment? A Betty Anne Waters commitment? A Rudy Ruettiger commitment?

Former NBA coach Pat Riley said, "There are only two options regarding commitment. You're either in or out. There's no such thing as a life in-between."

A master salesperson is all-in.

Are you?

16
Persistence

"Persistence is to the character of man as carbon is to steel."
Napoleon Hill (1883-1970)

Persistence is the everlasting implementation of your commitment. Persistence is hanging in there against Herculean odds, for as long as it takes, no matter the hardship endured. It's head butting against a wall of granite until finally it gives way and crumbles. Calvin Coolidge, 30th president of the United States, said, "Nothing in this world can take the place of persistence. Talent will not; nothing is more common than unsuccessful people with talent. Genius will not; unrewarded genius is almost a proverb. Education will not; the world is full of educated derelicts. Persistence and determination alone are omnipotent. The slogan 'press on' has solved and always will solve the problems of the human race."

Persistence is what will sustain you when adversity raises its jagged blade and stabs you in the heart. It matters not in the slightest how talented you are, or your track record up to that point—adversity *will* strike somewhere along the way to challenge you and your commitment, by and large when you least expect it. You must be prepared to face it with equanimity and poise.

Adversity Strikes

My time came in the spring of 1992, after being in the telephone-book-cover advertising business for 23 years. I was a master of my craft, but I wasn't nearly tough as I thought.

I was working Nashville, Tennessee. It took me 15 work-weeks—Monday through Wednesday—to complete a town in those days; adversity reared its ugly head in week number five. After two decades-plus of uncanny consistency, the losses suddenly started piling up like a stinking pyramid in a garbage dump. My 60% closing ratio nose-dived into the toilet. During weeks five through nine, I wrote a grand total of two sales. Three of those weeks I went blank; until Nashville, I'd had three blank weeks in 23 *years*.

I didn't have a clue what was causing this unprecedented collapse. It was as if an earthquake had struck and smashed my career to smithereens. Fear, the great enemy I had always laughed at, and challenged, suddenly gripped me like a vice. Doubt, fear's twin brother, crept into my psyche and poisoned my mind; I was consumed by the locusts of doom. My stomach in a constant state of upheaval, I began to have thoughts of leaving the business. The losses just kept piling up, burying me under an avalanche of baffling futility. I thought of myself as a .400 hitter; now I couldn't get a hit to save my life. I started pressing, which no doubt made things even worse. When you become desperate, that desperation curdles into a stench of fear the prospect smells like a bloodhound; and it repels him, turns him off completely.

The stress was so overwhelming that I suffered severe angina and underwent angioplasty to open up a blocked artery. I'm sure I brought my illness upon myself; desperation can do that to us—hyphenate "disease" and you get "dis-ease." I took nine weeks off to recover, grab hold of my sanity.

I went back into the field staring at six more weeks in Nashville. I made a commitment to relax and give it my all. I'd let the Powers That Be worry about results, I decided. I'd concentrate on proper execution, nothing else. I'd go back to selling fearlessly. The town soon would be over, and win, lose, or draw, I'd head to a new town and a fresh start.

It proved to be an excellent strategy: those six weeks were all highly productive, and although Nashville wasn't one of my more profitable towns, my fear of leaving the business turned out to be nothing more than imagination temporarily run amok, an interim blip in an otherwise consistent career. I never again experienced anything nigh to those five bizarre weeks in Nashville. It's true: what doesn't kill you makes you stronger. After Nashville, I knew I could handle anything.

Was I embarrassed that I crumbled so? Yes I was; I still am. However, as my son Jake likes to say, "Stuff happens," except he uses a different word. I know this, though: I would not have survived without the benefit of persistence. As President Coolidge said, it is omnipotent. And you won't survive without it either.

Fear Not the Storm

The negative emotions fear, doubt, and discouragement are hideous evils to be reckoned with. They'll sap every ounce of reason and strength within you, eat you alive like the E. coli virus. The only antidote to fear, doubt, and discouragement are positive emotions: courage, love, determination, and *persistence*.

If selling was as easy as snapping your fingers, they'd be lining up to do it. It isn't, though, and that's why it pays the big bucks it does. If you're persistent, if you hang in there during those tough times, you'll be worth every penny you're paid.

Have courage and fear not the storm, you'll be fine. A rainbow will appear and the sun will shine again.

17
Responsibility

"The buck stops here!"

Harry Truman (1884-1972)

It's become rather commonplace for a politician to stand before the press and say mea culpa for committing a gaffe or being unfaithful, for lying about his (or her) educational achievement or military service, or for engaging in some sort of sexual peccadillo. Often a distraught wife stands right next to her husband, in a staged display of support, even if he got caught with another woman.

Damage Control

What I find most curious about these "admissions of sin" is that their purpose is strictly damage control, not a true taking of responsibility. Oh, they utter the words, "I accept full responsibility," all right, but then fall back on a circumlocutory alibi to soft-pedal their responsibility.

"If I offended anyone, I sincerely apologize." What do you mean *if* you offended anyone? Why do you think you're standing up there, pal?

"The responsibility lies with me; however…" There isn't any *however*; you're up there because *you*, and only *you*, screwed up royal.

The point is this: We live in a world where people will say or do most anything to avoid responsibility for their irresponsible faux pas.

Lacking a Conscience

I once parked my field car on a side street in Oklahoma City, then gave a presentation at a meat market; when I returned, the car was "parked" in the middle of someone's lawn, the rear end smashed in. A witness told me an elderly couple had plowed into my car, viewed the damage, and then sped away like a Daytona 500 driver gunning out of a pit stop—no note, no apology, nada. Perhaps they didn't have insurance; they certainly didn't have a conscience.

My wife and I subscribe to the *Chicago Tribune*. It's rare that a week goes by without a story about a hit-and-run accident. Who leaves a bloodied victim to die in the street because of legal consequences? A lowlife who doesn't want to face responsibility for his actions: better to leave an "inconsequential stranger" to die than face shame and punishment. It's taking "every man for himself" to the level of tragedy.

There Are No Alibis

If you extend trust to a friend or relative and he betrays you, sells you out for the "right price" and is nasty about it to boot (an axiom of life is that guilty people often act hostile), would he have had the opportunity to betray you if you hadn't given that trust?

If you take on a partner and he absconds with all the money and the business fails, are *you* responsible, or will you simply tell the world what *he* did to you and walk away feeling absolved of responsibility in the matter? Who picked your partner? Who chose to trust him enough to go into business with him? You did—you, you, *you*.

Responsibility Begets Initiative

Thirty-five years ago I called on two service stations across the street from each other; the road they were on was under reconstruction, hardhats and heavy equipment everywhere—it looked like a gravel pit. I found the owner of the first station sitting dejectedly on a stoop, not another soul in sight. When I gave him my approach, he laughed bitterly and said, "Advertising? Are you kidding? Take a look at what they've done to me, man; my business is down to zilch because of all this lousy construction. I'll be forced out in about a month; know anybody who needs a good mechanic?"

When I went across the street, the owner came out from a repair bay holding a transmission dipstick, his uniform covered in grease. His response to my approach was 180 degrees different from the guy's across the street: "Advertising? Can't use any; can't get all the work done we've got now." He indicated the slew of cars parked outside awaiting service. "When I found out about all this construction and that it was gonna take a year and a half to complete, I went around the neighborhood knocking on doors, offering a bunch of specials to get enough business so we could get through this fiasco." He grinned like the Cheshire Cat, said, "Like I said, I've got more than I can handle. You can leave your card, though; if things ever slow up I'll give you a call."

Two men, two complete opposite levels of responsibility and initiative: one just accepted his fate; the other refused to. Keep them in mind when you face what seems like inevitable defeat. Maybe all you'll need to do is go knock on a few doors.

Who is responsible for *all* of *your* choices, decisions, and actions?

You are.

No Exceptions

A master salesperson is 100% responsible for *everything* that happens to him, every sale or loss. No matter how tempted you are to dump responsibility on some external factor, there is no blaming or alibiing. Don't do it, you'll only betray yourself.

It's your choice of vocation: the call was yours to make; you gave the presentation; if the prospect didn't buy, it's because you didn't close the sale. If you blame your company, your manager, your "lousy presentation," the weather, the recession, or offer up any of a thousand other lame excuses, you'll be spouting a lot of nonsense.

The responsibility is always yours.

There are no exceptions to this rule.

Don't just *accept* responsibility. *Be* responsible.

18
Competitiveness

"I love the competitiveness. I like to get out of the 'girl zone' and be a beast for a moment, to prove myself to people."
Elizabeth Kaiser

A master salesperson is highly competitive. She'll give twice as many presentations as normal to defeat her peers in a sales contest. Money motivates her, valuable prizes too, but not nearly so much as being able to say she's Top Banana in the company. She'll go to any lengths to be Number One. A sales contest can make the Stanley Cup finals seem like a little-old-lady pie-baking competition.

Team contests can produce an even higher level of competitiveness. They can become absolutely insane. I once met a man on a flight to Ontario, California—Tony, I never got his last name—who told me a great story about a team contest he'd participated in. Tony sold water conditioners.

Steak and Beans

"It was a six-week steak-and-bean contest," he told me. "Six weeks, no holds barred, of selling our water conditioners. Three three-man teams; the winners' prizes were $500, a three-day all-expenses-paid vacation for two in Las Vegas, and at the awards ceremony the best steak dinner money can buy."

"Per man?"

"Right."

"Please go on; I'm all ears."

"The losers got zip, zilch, in the way of prizes; and *their* dinner was a plate of baked beans—that was it, nothing but baked beans. Naturally, wives or girlfriends were exempt. They got steak, too."

Oh, this was vintage, I loved it.

"I've never experienced anything in my life like those six weeks," he said. "We plotted like the CIA. The three of us pushed each other to work harder and longer than any of us had ever thought possible. Our entire focus was on those other guys—the enemy—eating those beans while we celebrated with our steaks. That's all we thought about or talked about for six long weeks. Steak and beans, that was it; the rest of the world disappeared. My wife thought I'd gone loony-tunes. After all was said and done, we worked the kind of hours we normally never would've even *considered*; we earned commissions *far* beyond what was typical—I mean we're talking about a lot of money. The prize money and vacation to Vegas were great, the steak tasted like it was prepared for the gods, but the only thing that really mattered was those six bums choking on their beans."

We both started laughing.

"It was *glorious*, man. It was *uproarious*. It was wonderful. I never enjoyed winning anything so much in my entire life."

It sounded as sweet as "The Mound Road Story," or Michael Jordan sinking the winning shot against the Utah Jazz to win the NBA championship—the "shot" and the "pose." I sat there envious of Tony: oh how I wished I could have competed in *that* sales contest.

Competition Is Half the Fun

If you're not competitive, if you find ding-dong rivalry distasteful, a threat to your ego, you don't belong in sales. Competition is half the fun of the job.

Other than professional sports, I can't imagine a more satisfying way to make a living.

Be competitive and have a ball.

I hope you win—unless you really like beans.

19
Cold Calling

*"Courage is being scared to death—
but saddling up anyway."*
John Wayne (1907-1979)

If you've ever perused sales-job ads, you've probably noticed that many of them promise "leads, leads, leads—no cold calling." Even successful salespeople can be terrified of cold calling; they freeze up like a Popsicle at the thought of it. It's the one aspect of selling that is detested more than any other, by men and women alike. They'll do anything to avoid cold calling. You'd think they were being asked to slink unarmed into a dark grizzly-bear cave.

A friend of mine for 53 years, David Samson, runs an insurance agency with his son Ken. At a Cubs game last year, he admitted he doesn't cold call, even though he thinks he should (fortunately he doesn't have to since Dasco Insurance is a highly successful agency). Dave's a Pro who has plenty of company when it comes to cold calling.

A Sporting Event

I find the fear of cold calling amusing. Remember: If you think you can, or if you think you can't, you're right.

I spent 40 years doing 95% of my approaches via cold calling, 25 years *on the telephone*. There was nothing to it—a piece of cake. Sure, you must possess an armor-plated mental attitude to ward off all the "rejection," to say nothing of occasional hostility; but for the Pro who understands that no's matter not at all, only the yes's count, cold calling is a sporting event. It's a numbers game. We'll get into the numbers game in Part III, Work Habits.

Why are salespeople so afraid of cold calling? It's fear of the unknown, fear of strangers, and fear of rejection: the imagination run amok.

It's Only Business

Like the gangsters say: "It's only business." There isn't anything personal about it, except in your imagination. What we're talking about is a self-limiting belief. It can be rewired as easily as changing your clothes. You have a choice to make. Are you going to control your mind, or is your mind going to control you? Which is it?

Cold calling is like anything else in life: once you challenge yourself, *believe* you can do it, break the ice and keep succeeding, it becomes part of your comfort zone and is forever yours.

Doesn't it make sense to exponentially expand your galaxy of prospects? Why sit around twiddling your thumbs when you can be working? When you possess the wherewithal to cold call, anyone is fair game; you can open up the telephone book if you want to. The word "prospecting" won't have to be part of your selling lexicon; it was never part of mine.

Be a salesperson who isn't afraid to cold call and you'll be a Green Beret of selling and on the path to becoming a master. You'll truly be selling fearlessly.

20

Protecting Your Mental Attitude

"Your own mind is a sacred enclosure
into which nothing harmful can enter
except by your permission."
Ralph Waldo Emerson (1803-1882)

There are two kinds of presentation losses you must protect yourself against or you're just begging for a kick to the groin of your mental attitude.

Kissed Out the Door

The first is when the prospect kisses you out the door. That's what a Pro calls it—"kissed out the door." The prospect said no, but wants you to know what a *terrific* salesperson you are. He's handing you a Pyrrhic victory to soften the blow of turning you down; he thinks it'll make both of you feel better. He means well, perhaps even believes his "compliment" to be true, just not enough to sign the contract.

The problem is, if you accept his "compliment," you're allowing *him* to take responsibility for the no-sale, instead of shouldering it yourself. If you couldn't close the sale, you didn't achieve your purpose for being there; and if you walk out that door all tingly and aglow because of nice things he said about you, you're gullible as a two-year-old who had his eye on Mommy's purse, right up until she dangled the distraction of her keys.

The prospect is insulting your intelligence. What's worse, if you accept his kiss out the door, your selling resolve has been knocked to the canvas for an eight count—next time you won't battle quite as hard or hang in there nearly as long.

I refused to be kissed out the door. The rule was inviolable as a citadel: no left-handed "compliments," thank you very much. The dialogue usually went like this:

"You're a terrific salesman, Bob, one of the best I ever met."

"Not this time, I wasn't."

"No, no, I really mean it, you gave a great presentation."

"Really, then why did you turn me down?"

Now he's on the spot; this is when you'll either get his true reason—one you can rebut and close on—or some hemming and hawing, nothing concrete to work with. Even if you don't close the sale, you can hold your head high because you refused the disingenuous "compliment" and didn't allow him to kiss you out the door.

You protected your mental attitude for the next call.

Gratuitous Cheap Shots

The second kind of loss you must guard against is when the prospect gratuitously tears down your product or service, or worse, you personally. This guy not only isn't buying from you, but wants to wound you, destroy your mental attitude. He wants to rip apart the very fabric of your self-esteem. He thrives on chewing his fellow man to pieces, especially salespeople; it's sport to him. He's an unhappy fellow and misery loves company, doesn't it?

Over the years I met quite a number of these piranhas. I never allowed them to get away with their pugnacity. I'd stand toe to toe with them and throw it right back in their faces; however, always politely, with a warm smile for affect.

If, say, he owned a hardware store, I'd say something like, "The covers will be out in March; ask the hardware store that's on there how well it worked for them—I think you'll hear a lot of positive things." My meaning was not subtle. I defended the quality of my service and had the pleasure of letting him know he wasn't the only hardware store in town, one of his competitors would be in the space he was disparaging.

I walked out with my head held high and my strong belief in my service intact. It was the prospect who was left doubting himself, and possibly fearful that his toughest competitor would get an edge on him. After being the target of his gratuitous cheap shot, I considered him deserving of my retort.

If a prospect didn't buy but was cordial and respectful, I always responded in kind and so should you—everyone has the right to say no.

But not the right to gratuitously tear down you or your product or service. Don't ever allow it.

Your mental attitude must be protected at all cost.

On to the next.

21
The Devil's Retirement Story

"We are each our own devil,
and we make this world our hell."
Oscar Wilde (1854-1900)

The first time I heard Earl Nightingale's melodious voice was at a sales meeting while training to become a telephone-book-cover advertising salesman. The tape recorder lay atop the hotel conference room table and six of us listened intently: it was "Acres of Diamonds," from "Lead the Field." Trudeau owned a complete set of "Lead the Field." He played a tape at every sales meeting to start things off with an inspiring message. "Lead the Field" still is available by Nightingale-Conant; in my opinion, you'll never listen to anything more inspirational.

Mr. Nightingale's deep hypnotic voice and language agility put him right up there with the great communicators of his time: he had the power of Billy Graham, sans the preaching; the trustworthiness of Walter Cronkite; and the inspiration of Winston Churchill. I loved listening to him. His eloquence was the equivalent of Luciano Pavarotti singing "Nessun Dorma."

"The Devil's Wedge"

I was driving one afternoon a year after that sales meeting when an Earl Nightingale radiobroadcast entitled "The Devil's Wedge" came on the radio. "The Devil's Wedge" was taken from an old fable, *The Devil's Best Tool*, that Mr. Nightingale used to make his point, which hit me like a thunderbolt and has stayed with me all these years.

Soon after, I created my own version of the fable's premise: the Devil selling his tools of the trade. I've told the story dozens of times over the decades, often on airplanes and usually to someone I sensed was down in the dumps. I hope you like it.

Eternity Is a Long Time

The Devil—also known as Beelzebub, Satan, Lucifer, Prince of Darkness, or any one of 38 other monikers—had been in the business of tormenting mankind since the origin of man's reign on earth. Business never slowed, and he was wealthy beyond human imagination. His tools, the weapons of his trade, were all the negative emotions that had escaped from Pandora's Box into his gleeful clutches—anger, hatred, fear, jealousy, revenge, greed, superstition, envy, doubt, worry, and a host of poisonous others. He had a monopoly. He used these corrosive toxins to destroy man at every opportunity, and to say he enjoyed his work would be the biggest understatement of all time—he relished it.

However, eternity is a long time, and after countless millennia the Devil became bored with doing the same old same old, over and over and *over* again, and contemplated retirement. He possessed wealth far beyond his eternal needs, and if the business wasn't fun anymore, why keep at it? He owned a plush 10,000-acre resort in the Caribbean that rivaled Atlantis, and perhaps it was time to kick back and enjoy the fruits of his toil: some deep-sea fishing; golf; world travel for enjoyment instead of business; food fit for the gods, prepared by a team of four-star chefs; the largest library in the world; a team of masseuses; plus an endless list of other goodies. It sounded perfect.

Evil Angels

There were a bunch of evil angels working upstairs for the competition. For centuries they had tried to buy into the tormenting-mankind business, but were stymied by the Devil's refusal to part with any of his destructive weapons. He was confident he'd have no difficulty finding buyers for these torturous thorns-in-the-heart of mankind, no difficulty at all.

It came to pass that the Devil conducted an auction and, one to each evil angel, sold off all the banes of Pandora's Box.

Numero Uno

He sold them all except one, the one he called Numero Uno, far and away the most powerful of the lot. It was the one that, after all others had proved ineffective, *never* failed to bring man to his suffering knees. No way would he part with Numero Uno. He would keep it as an insurance policy: What if retirement didn't suit him? What if he missed the action and wanted to return to the business? By keeping Numero Uno, he'd have something to fall back on—the deadliest of the deadly. So he placed Numero Uno in a safe deposit box where it remained hidden and dormant, and for a spell of time man stood at the pinnacle of his reign—never happier, never more prosperous, and never more spiritually content.

Oh, the evil angels were out there, all right, plying their new trade, with all the fury of a lynch mob. Man still suffered from their attacks, but with Numero Uno out of the picture, things were hardly catastrophic. All things considered, it truly was the best of times.

For a number of years the Devil enjoyed his retirement; so did the evil angels, who competed with each other the same cutthroat way other businesses do—telecommunication companies, for example.

Boredom

Everything was fine right up until the Devil had his Great Epiphany and realized, hey, this easy living had been great for a while, but an eternity of it wasn't for him, thank you very much. The ennui he'd felt before retirement was now in the distant past, and now he missed the action more than he could bear. He rented an office, got good old Numero Uno out of the safe deposit box, dusted it off, and got back on the bicycle, so to speak, and went right back into the business of tormenting man.

Man's golden age was over quicker than you could say "The Devil made me do it."

The evil angels cried foul. Collectively they possessed far more weapons than the Devil (quantity, that is, not quality), but alas, they couldn't compete. Numero Uno was far more powerful *all by itself* than all their weapons *put together*. It was like a junior high football team versus the New England Patriots; Goldwater trying to unseat Johnson in 1964; the Duchy of Grand Fenwick at war with the United States of America in *The Mouse That Roared.*

It was no contest.

Full Circle

After the dust settled, the evil angels begged the Devil to buy them out, at a loss, of course, which he gladly did. Everything had come full circle and the Devil once again was the sole tormenter of man. The evil angels, wings in hand, went back upstairs and asked for their old jobs back, got them—forgiveness is standard in Heaven—and never again attempted to get back into the tormenting business.

They'd had *everything but* Numero Uno, but it hadn't been nearly enough; the Devil had *only* Numero Uno, but it was more than enough.

Numero Uno, the poison that is to man what kryptonite is to Superman.

Numero Uno, the worst calamity that can befall man.

What do *you* think it is?

Nothing so Paralyzing

D-i-s-c-o-u-r-a-g-e-m-e-n-t. (In the original fable it was the Wedge of Discouragement.) Like a malignant tumor, one naked-to-the-eye cell of it metastasizes until your spirit dies and awaits burial. You're finished, *kaput*. All the other negative emotions—fear, hatred, jealousy, envy, revenge, anger, greed, superstition, doubt, worry—will lead you to take action, albeit not necessarily constructive action; but discouragement begets self-pity, which freezes you up like a catatonic schizophrenic in a mental ward. It immobilizes you—you sit and mope in a cloud of despairing inertia, you do nothing but ponder the terms of your surrender.

Discouragement was the Devil's weapon of choice when he attacked me during those five ugly weeks in Nashville. He came at me with good old Numero Uno and, I'm embarrassed to say, he almost got me, that's how vulnerable man is to discouragement, even the normally mentally strong. Getting past that dark episode is as satisfying to me as surviving kidney cancer.

If (when) it happens to you, recognize it for what it is and battle it with all you've got. It's an illusion designed to trick you into full submission.

Send the Devil packing and be of good cheer.

PART III

WORK HABITS

22
Work Schedule

"He who every morning plans the transaction of the day and follows out that plan, carries a thread that will guide him through the maze of the most busy life. But where no plan is laid, where the disposal of time is surrendered merely to the chance of incidence, chaos will soon reign."

Victor Hugo (1802-1885)

A straight-commission salesperson may work as much or little as he chooses to, depending on how hungry he is. Some companies are stricter than others, but usually it's the salesperson's decision. He knows how much he needs to earn and what it's going to take to consistently attain his goal.

For a disciplined salesperson, this prerogative is utopia; for an undisciplined salesperson, it's a ticket into the abyss of doom. After I left the real estate business, I discovered there was a *huge* difference between shooting the breeze with colleagues and actually working. I discussed this with my father, who said, "When you work, you work; when you play, you play."

Canon for 40 Years

I took my father's words to heart and after that there was no in-between. When it was time to work, that's what I did—that's all I did. If you're not preparing diligently, making calls, setting up appointments, or giving presentations, you're not working; how "busy" you are is irrelevant (see Chapter 23, "Self-Starter").

Foundation of Work Habits

The foundation of a salesperson's work habits is the work schedule—definitive set hours or number of presentations, on explicit days of the week. The work schedule must be established and adhered to, no matter what. Throughout my career I had a number of work schedules; the last 10 years it was as follows:

On Sunday I flew to the town I was working. On Monday I made my appointment calls—I was on the telephone from 9:00 a.m. to 11:30 a.m., took lunch from 11:30 a.m. to 1:00 p.m., and then continued making calls until 4:00 p.m. When I filled my eight appointment slots—four Tuesday and four Wednesday—before 4:00 p.m., my day was over early; on the rare occasions that I didn't fill my eight slots by 4:00 p.m., I often made additional calls until I met my goal, but that was optional. On Tuesday and Wednesday my work was not completed until I'd given the last presentation, no matter the hour. My week ended after Wednesday's final presentation. I flew home Thursday morning. I did this 35 to 40 weeks a year.

Time versus Money

My dear friend and accountant Dave Levinson used to say I had the best part-time job in the world. He forgot I was running a business, too. When I returned home there were a multitude of other tasks to deal with. His point was that I could have put in more field time, which would have meant more income, but from my perspective I already was earning far more than I'd ever dreamed possible as a younger man, and time with my family was more important than more money. This is a subjective decision each salesperson must make for himself.

It's Sacred

Know this though: my work schedule was set in reinforced concrete and tempered steel. It could be 3:30 on a Monday afternoon and I was mentally and physically exhausted, crawling on my hands and knees in a 130 degree desert towards the oasis, dying to call it a day; but I would not—*never once*—give in, disrespect the rules of my sacred work schedule.

This may seem too inflexible to you. To each his own. If you think my work-schedule discipline is too harsh, too rigid, so be it; you need to make your own decisions about *your* work schedule. But as Miss Sullivan used to say, "A word to the wise": that iron-clad discipline worked for me and it'll definitely work for you, too. Anything less I can't guarantee.

It would behoove you to remember my father's advice, too—"When you work, you work; when you play, you play." Keep them compartmentalized; never allow them to trespass across each other's boundaries. This will serve you well.

A master salesperson works according to a set schedule.

The easy part is you get to design that schedule; the hard part is you may not cheat, *no matter what.*

23
Self-Starter

"Plans are only good intentions unless they immediately degenerate into hard work."
Peter Drucker (1909-2005)

Peruse sales want ads and you'll see "self-starter" in many. A self-starter does the work without needing to be told to.

Microwave-Oven Business

Thirty-eight years ago my father got the "bright" idea of going into the direct-to-the-consumer microwave-oven business; it was a franchise from a major corporation. He asked me to join him in this venture. I reluctantly agreed, but on a limited basis. My focus was on my advertising business, and I really didn't have the time or inclination for another venture.

Logistics

Dad rented an office on Milwaukee Avenue in Chicago, furnished it, and took steps to hire a sales manager to run the show. We rattled through *four* of them in six months; we burned through 25 to 30 salespeople, as well. No one, it seemed, was in a great hurry to actually *sell* microwave ovens. The few times I popped in, usually on a Friday when I wasn't on the road, the guys would be sitting around, coffee cups in hand, talking a grand game, but actual presentations were few and far between. Mighty Casey struck out; these guys weren't even grabbing a bat. It was driving me nuts. I'll admit, though: if I'd been asked to lug a 70-pound microwave oven up and down three flights of stairs, I would have said "No thank you" so fast my father's agape mouth could've swallowed an entire beehive. I could barely lift the damn thing, let alone carry it 10 feet.

We were hemorrhaging money on this deal like blood spurting out of a torn aorta. I told my father discretion was the better part of valor and suggested that we chalk this endeavor up to posterity, but he wanted to try one more manager/salesperson to see if he could make this white elephant fly.

Randy

The young man he hired next was in his mid-20s, clean-cut, lanky, and according to Dad, "Ready to set the world on fire." I hoped he would just sell a few microwave ovens. We'll call him Randy.

The first two weeks, Randy redecorated the entire office. He did a fabulous job painting every inch of the place, including the bathroom. He explained that we needed an office he and the "other salespeople" could be proud of. When I asked about following up on leads, giving presentations, he promised he would begin as soon as "everything else was taken care of."

Hmmmm…

The third week, Randy bought a new T-Bird. The negotiations with the dealer took several days. Randy was quite excited—it was a beautiful car, befitting his new title, General Manager. He explained that now he could pull up to a prospect's abode with a certain sense of pride; who wanted to buy a microwave oven from a salesperson driving a beat-up old jalopy?

Okay…

The fourth week, Randy began extensive studying: he was determined to know everything possible about microwave ovens. The kid really hit the books; he could tell you anything you wanted to know about our microwave oven, and microwave-oven cooking. He was a veritable walking, talking microwave-oven encyclopedia.

It was impressive, it really was.

It was preparation at its finest—sans the execution. Every time I brought up *selling* microwave ovens, he was just "a short step away" from getting started.

Oy.

"Oh ye of little faith," my father said.

The fifth week, Randy was stricken ill. All those paint and turpentine fumes had done him in.

Midway through the sixth week, Randy got "a better offer" and quit, drove off in his shiny new T-Bird, never to be seen or heard from again.

My father's philosophy was "When you work, you work; when you play, you play." Randy's philosophy was "Get ready, get set...get ready, get set...get ready, get set..."

The good news is that we finally closed the business.

Delusional Hogwash

A salesperson makes calls, sets appointments, gives presentations, and *sells*. Anything that takes precedence is delusional hogwash.

If you don't want to make calls, set appointments, give presentations, and *sell*, pick another line of work. You'll save yourself and your employer a lot of needless disappointment.

A master salesperson is a self-starter; he knows what to do and does it without being told to.

24
Chunks

"The whole is more
than the sum of its parts."
Aristotle (384 BC-322 BC)

The main reason so many dreams go unfulfilled is because we tend to view the whole, instead of breaking it up into manageable chunks. A man desires to write a novel, but what's staring him in the face is the daunting task of creating 500 pages of narrative, perhaps a year's work, when all he should be thinking about is the opening sentence. This agonizing over the whole enchilada, instead of slicing it up into edible bites, overwhelms us and is the root cause of most of the procrastination we beat ourselves up over. Eventually it leads to surrender, to the pity of "what might have been." Sad words indeed. John Greenleaf Whittier said it so well:

> For all sad words of tongue and pen,
> The saddest are these,
> "It might have been."

Chunks Add Up to a Successful Whole

If you had 400 one-pound weights and you needed to move them from one room to another, would you place them in a single container and try to move all 400 in one fell swoop, or would you move them in smaller, lighter loads? It's a no-brainer, isn't it?

A new building is constructed one floor at a time.

A retirement fund grows each year with additional principal and compounded interest.

A seven-course dinner is served one course at a time.

A movie is shot one scene at a time.

The Chicago Blackhawks won the 2010 Stanley Cup by winning four hockey games in four separate series—16 triumphant chunks of the best hockey you'll ever see.

Work in Chunks

I worked in chunks, never the whole, and that's how you should approach it, too. You'll have daily, weekly, monthly, and yearly goals, but the only thing you should be thinking about is the presentation at hand. Tomorrow is another day. The week will end soon enough, so too the month and year. Each presentation will be a chunk of each goal. Ten presentations a week for 50 weeks add up to 500 for the year; with that many at-bats, I guarantee you'll bring in a lot of runs.

If you don't like "chunks," pick your own word: parts, portions, fractions, shares, subdivisions, pieces, segments, chapters—whatever is your pleasure. What matters is that you keep your perspective narrowly focused where it belongs: on the next presentation.

Maintaining the discipline of working in chunks will serve you well.

25
Consistency

"My goal in sailing isn't to be brilliant or flashy in individual races, just to be consistent over the long run."

Dennis Connor

The mark of a master salesperson's work habits is consistency; inconsistency is the hobgoblin of the master pretender.

Keith

In Chapter 4, "Do You Have to Believe in Your Product or Service?" I spoke of an eminently talented salesman, Keith. Trudeau had a love/hate relationship with Keith, who when motivated could sell advertising like Jascha Heifetz played the violin. The problem was that he was rarely motivated. Think of the Hare in Aesop's fable *The Tortoise and the Hare* and you'll have Keith down to a "T". He did not overly tax himself.

Except during a sales contest, a biannual event. Keith was super-competitive; he wore his top-producer crown proudly and was loath to surrender it to anyone else. When he competed in the nine-week contests, his pride was on the line and he morphed into a monster salesman, tripling his normal dollar volume *in the final six weeks*; the first three weeks he was the Hare napping on the ground. This boggled my rookie mind. I was in awe of his ability, but it troubled me that a man with such incredible selling prowess was so inconsistent.

I recall having lunch with Trudeau, listening to him rant about Keith's lackadaisical, irreverent ways. It frustrated Trudeau that Keith couldn't be motivated without a sales contest, and even then did only as much as necessary to win; Trudeau felt taken advantage of. I sympathize with him; I've dealt with my own versions of Keith. You know you're getting your pocket picked, but there's not a darn thing you can do about it.

It's frustrating, baffling, *maddening* to sit back and watch a top-tier talent run hot and cold. To re-quote Calvin Coolidge, "Nothing is more common than unsuccessful people with talent." Inconsistent talent is as wasteful as grinding chateaubriand into hamburger.

Debt of Gratitude

Looking back, I owe Keith a huge debt of gratitude for showing me how *not* to be the salesperson I desired to be. The Hare displayed bursts of greatness, but the Tortoise won the race. I take pride in all aspects of my selling career, but none more than 40 years—sans five weeks—of unyielding consistency. "When you work, you work," my father said, and when I was in the field, I always gave it everything I had, held nothing back.

Keith left the company two years before I did; I never saw him again. I have few regrets in my career, but one is that I never got to compete against him when I no longer was a rookie, when I was at the top of my game. It would have been fun and, I believe, quite gratifying.

Pete Rose

I'm not an admirer of Pete Rose, but I respect the consistent way he played the game. You don't get 4,256 lifetime hits—a record—by being inconsistent. Check out his hit totals from 1963 through 1984—we'll chalk up 1985 and 1986 to his age, 44 and 45, ancient for baseball:

1963: 170	1964: 139	1965: 209	1966: 205	1967: 176
1968: 210	1969: 218	1970: 205	1971: 192	1972: 198
1973: 230	1974: 185	1975: 210	1976: 215	1977: 204
1978: 198	1979: 208	1980: 185	1981: 140	1982: 172
1983: 121	1984: 214			

Rose's consistency mirrored his hustle—no pun intended.

Greg Maddux

A baseball player I *do* admire is Greg Maddux. Talk about consistency: from 1988 through 2004, *17 straight years*, the man won at least 15 games. He is the only pitcher in baseball history to accomplish that stupendous feat. He won four Cy Young Awards *in a row*. His 18 Gold Gloves are the most ever for *any* position. When he's voted into the Baseball Hall of Fame, I'll raise a glass to Mr. Maddux.

Be the Tortoise

Remember, the Tortoise won the race. If you're not consistently selling at full throttle, your work habits are suffering from a lack of character. Don't cheat your family; don't cheat your company; don't cheat your colleagues; but most important, don't cheat yourself. Put in the requisite time in the field, be the best you can be every day of your selling life. Anything less and you're committing a sin.

If you consistently give your best, success will consistently be yours.

26
Saturation Point

"He that has satisfied his thirst turns his back on the well."
Baltasar Gracian (1601-1658)

Every salesperson has weekly, monthly, and yearly income targets to shoot for, and it's vital that she hits them. So much is at stake: money, ego, status in the company, rank amongst colleagues, peace of mind, that new vacation home in the Upper Peninsula. The target numbers are embedded in her subconscious, constantly popping into her conscious mind, reminding her of what she must accomplish.

Feeling No Pain

Let's say her weekly target is $15,000 sales volume, $5,000 income—if your remuneration percentage is greater than 33%, you're doing better than most. She hits her target Wednesday, on her final presentation of the day. Wow, the week is *really* looking sky blue, and just think—she has two more days to pile it on, rocket that number into outer space; she's feeling no pain. As the Greeks would say, *OOMPAH*!

Everything is bright and shiny, right?

Well, not entirely…

Just Gravy

You see, she's reached her saturation point, too—the level at which her subconscious tells her any more business this week is just gravy. Oh, she daydreams about more, but if she goes blank Thursday and Friday, what would be so terrible? She's *there*, man. That glow she's feeling is a narcotic numbing her hunger. It's such a comfy feeling, like sleeping in on a cool Sunday morning. More business would be lovely, but she doesn't *need* it like she needed that first $5,000, which is comfortably safe on the scoreboard. She'll continue presenting Thursday and Friday, but won't push quite as hard or hang in there as long. The worst part is that she won't consciously be aware of it.

It's Universal

Every salesperson has her saturation point; it's a law of Mother Selling Nature. The trick is to be aware so you can *try* to combat it.

Good luck with that. "It's not *nice* to fool Mother Nature"—or so the Chiffon margarine commercials told us.

Did I have a saturation point?

Yes I did; however, I like to think my work-schedule discipline and killer instinct insulated me from its aftermath. (We'll discuss killer instinct in Part IV, Chapter 42.)

Think of a saturation point as a subtle headwind, which picks up strength as your earnings increase.

It isn't deadly as Achilles' heel, but it *is* a chink in your armor. My mother used to say, "To be forewarned is to be forearmed."

When you're ahead it's time to pour it on!

27
Common-Sense Basics

"The three great essentials to achieve anything worthwhile are, first, hard work; second, stick-to-itiveness; third, common sense."

Thomas Alva Edison (1847-1931)

A month before my 13th birthday my parents took me to Baer Brothers and Prodie, an apparel store on Chicago's far Westside. The purpose of this shopping trip was a Bar Mitzvah suit for yours truly. I'll never forget the salesman who waited on us. Not because of his appearance—early 50s, about five-foot eleven, balding, hefty, well dressed in a suit and tie. Not because of his personality, which was pleasant enough. No, he's indelibly etched in my memory because his stinking breath could've killed Dumbo at 40 paces.

Mouthwash and Breath Mints

He and his rancid breath were all over me like black on licorice; no matter how I twisted and turned to get away from him, held my breath till I turned blue, there was no escape. He was there to assist us and he took his job seriously. He helped me on with the jackets, kept tugging at the lapels, shoulders, and trousers, all the while talking a blue streak to me and my parents. Every whiff of the man made me want to retch; I came close a couple of times. It was a sickening experience. My parents never knew why I was so surly that day.

Common sense should tell you: keep some mouthwash and breath mints in your car and use them.

Showers and Deodorant

I've sat next to people on airplanes who hadn't bathed in days, their body odor foul as a skunk's. It's torture. Prospects will rid themselves of you faster than Usain Bolt runs the 100-meter dash if you have body odor. The only antidote is lots of soap and water—it's called a shower, and you should take one every morning before putting on fresh deodorant. If you think you're the holy exception to this rule, you're dumber than someone who still believes the earth is flat.

Suit and Tie

I always worked in a suit and tie, no matter how hot it was or how casually my prospects dressed. I considered it a matter of respect. A State Farm agent in northern California once said, "I knew I was buying from you the second you walked in here wearing that suit and tie. That's unheard of around here. I can't tell you how much I respect that."

I recommend you dress like a professional: wear a suit and tie. It won't score points with everyone, but it *will* with certain prospects.

Punctuality

The biggest no-brainer of all is *always be punctual*. Never waste another man's time unless you have a damn good excuse: car accident, flat tire, someone became ill or died, you became ill, your last presentation ran late. As the wife said to her thickheaded husband, "You couldn't call?" You have a cell phone. There is no excuse, *none whatsoever*, for not calling and letting a prospect know you're running late or have to reschedule. If you waltz in offering no apology, no explanation, you'll be resented, and starting out with a prospect who resents you is at best an uphill battle.

Car Washes

How do you react to a filthy car? Personally, it turns me off and I'm not alone. Prospects will judge you by the cleanliness and condition of your car. Pull up in a dirty, messy, banged-up car and you'll be seen in the same light. A carwash is an investment that pays multiple dividends. Get your car washed.

Selling and Alcohol Don't Mix

Call on a prospect with booze on your breath and you're inviting disaster. Don't do it. It's worse than bad breath. If you're compelled to have a drink or two at a business lunch, wait until you're clear-headed enough to make that next call and use your mouthwash. There's no exception to this rule.

Respect

These common-sense basics boil down to one thing: respect for the people you do business with. Think of them in terms of the Golden Rule: "Do unto others as you would have them do unto you." If you flout these basics, the costs in lost sales and commissions will be staggering. You'll be committing economic hari-kari.

Use some common sense.

Be a stickler for the basics.

28
Working Smart

"Working hard and working smart sometimes can be two different things."

Byron Dorgan

Working smart means wringing maximum production from your work schedule. It's coming up with new ideas to bring that about. Working hard without working smart is as foolish as carving the Thanksgiving turkey with a dull knife instead of the electric knife your wife just bought you.

The First 15 Years

Every business has ways to work smart. In the first 15 years of my advertising career, I called on owners in person at their businesses. I prepared the night before by organizing prospects into a stack of 50 index cards, in a closest-to-the-next route. The next day I drove around making my calls; this led to immediate presentations and setting appointments. The index cards and closest-to-the-next route, at the time, were examples of working smart.

Change One

After those first 15 years, about twenty-five years ago, I decided to make my calls on the telephone to increase call volume. The idea intrigued me so much I gave it a four-week test run. I was bucking the old adage "If it isn't broke, don't fix it," especially since a telephone approach is much easier for a prospect to blow off than a face-to-face encounter. The telephone demands superior rebutting skills and voice presence than in-person interaction. The experiment worked: I significantly increased presentations, which produced a higher dollar volume. I found a way to work more productively, to work smarter. The index cards and closest-to-the-next route went by the wayside. I worked this way for another 15 years.

Change Two

Ten years ago I made a second change. This time I opted to devote Monday strictly to setting up appointments for Tuesday and Wednesday. Once again I gave it a four-week trial run, which proved successful. The number of presentations increased. I had found a way to work even smarter.

The three-stage 30-year process was like candlelight to gas to electricity: each step enabled me to be more productive.

Multiple Counts

Before 1980 I worked midsize towns like Kalamazoo, Michigan, and Lima, Ohio. I did 5,000 counts: the number of telephone-book-covers mailed to upscale homeowners. Then I got the idea of doing *multiple* 5,000 counts in cities like Lexington, Kentucky, and Tucson, Arizona. Depending on the size of the city, I did four to six sections—20,000 to 30,000 total counts. I more than *quadrupled* my income. If an idea could be framed and mounted, that one would be hanging prominently in the Louvre. The only downside: I had to fly to work, which meant leaving Sunday instead of early Monday morning—a sacrifice I'd make again in a heartbeat.

When to Call on a Business

There were other work-smart considerations in my business; for example, *when* to call on a particular type of business. Call on a beauty salon after Wednesday and your chances of speaking to the owner are remote. Call on an auto repair shop early in the morning when customers are dropping off cars or late-afternoon when they're picking up their cars, and your odds of success diminish greatly. Here are a few other examples of when not to call on a business: a florist during Valentine's Day week, Mother's Day week, Thanksgiving week, or the Christmas season; a real estate salesperson on Tuesday mornings, it's usually when she's out on caravan inspecting new listings; a heating/air conditioning contractor on a 100 degree day in mid-August; a tax preparer between January and April 15th; a caterer or restaurant from 11:00 a.m. to 2:00 p.m.

Flout any of these timing taboos and you'll be spinning your wheels. You'll be working dumb instead of smart.

Time Mismanagement

Have you ever visited an automobile dealership for service and observed a group of salespeople standing around shooting the breeze? There isn't a single customer in the showroom and they don't have a thing to do. I pity their lack of initiative. If I were a car salesperson, I'd be on the telephone during that "downtime" calling potential customers from hot lists; but then I'm used to calling on people, not waiting for them to drop in.

Referrals

An essential part of working smart is asking for referrals; a referral is worth a pitcher full of cold calls, and your closing percentage will rise proportionately when you're presenting from referrals. This is how I asked for referrals after I made a sale:

"Ben, may I ask a huge favor?" People will go out of their way to assist you if you ask for help.

"Sure, what is it?"

"Our most effective way of calling on businesses is by referral. Are there any businesspeople you know personally, that you feel good about, whom you think we could serve effectively? Anyone you can think of; I can't begin to tell you how important referrals are to us." I succeeded two out of three times, and when

I did I always asked permission to use the client's name with each referral he'd given me.

Never walk out of a sale without asking for referrals.

New Ideas

There are always smarter ways to work, if you're on the lookout and willing to challenge conventional wisdom. Sometimes a tiny tweak can make a *huge* difference. George Bernard Shaw said, "Some men see things as they are and ask why. Others dream things that never were and ask why not."

My friend Barry Thalden, the architect I spoke of in the Introduction, has been in business 38 years and is constantly searching for new ideas to make his company's presentations more effective.

I encourage you to do the same.

Be on the lookout for opportunities to work smart. Concentrate, analyze. A new idea can be worth a fortune in additional sales.

29
Callbacks

"It has been my observation that most people get ahead during the time that others waste time."
Henry Ford (1863-1947)

There are salespeople in businesses that require multiple calls, in order to close a sale: a Boeing rep selling airplanes to a major airline; an architecture firm selling a plan for a hotel and casino; a software salesperson selling a revolutionary new program to General Electric. Close to half of all salespeople, though, are one-call-close simple-sale salespeople. I was a one-call-close simple-sale salesperson. Callbacks—when a prospect says he'll think it over and asks you to call him back—were considered the curse of the black plague. Automobile and other store salespeople refer to them as "bebacks." I refused to accept them because only one out of 30 turned into a sale.

Slim to None

When a prospect can't be closed immediately after the presentation, the odds are slim to none that he'll close himself a day or two later when the full power of the presentation has faded from memory. Should he ask someone else's opinion—someone who did not have benefit of the presentation—he'll likely get a negative slant. From the prospect's perspective, it's simply easier *not* to take a risk and buy.

In 40 years I sold maybe 25 callbacks; 25 sales out of over 12,000 presentations, and the only reason I sold those 25 was because the prospects called *me* back.

Reverse Direction

When a prospect said, "I want to think it over, call me back tomorrow," and I felt rebutting any further would be a waste of time,

I produced another business card and politely explained why I wasn't going to call him back, but certainly would welcome *his* call and his business *if* he wanted the ad space, *and if it was still available*. This was a shot of reverse direction (see Part IV, Chapter 51, "Reverse Direction"). If he didn't want the space, I told him no explanation was necessary. My refusal to call back angered about one out of five prospects and the "sale" died on the spot, which didn't bother me because a callback was a millimeter beyond worthless anyway. Some prospects encouraged me to call back by attempting to sell me the idea that they were seriously contemplating my proposal and chances were excellent they'd be the exception to the one-out-of-30 rule. I'd smile, say, "I hope so," but held my ground: they could call *me* back *if* they were so inclined, and *if the space was still available*.

No Regrets

Did I lose a few sales by taking this tack? I'm sure I did, but with no regrets. I would do it the same way today and recommend you do, too. Why waste your precious time on a one-out-of-30 long shot when your closing percentage is 60%? You do the math: it's like comparing a bushel full of apples to one that accidentally fell from the tree. Why get your hopes up and why put your mental attitude on the line to hear no again 29 out of 30 times? Why start tomorrow off with a no before you even hit the field? Chances are good, too, it won't be just one callback he'll ask you to make; uh-uh, there are prospects who will keep putting you off until my Cubbies win a World Series. The occasional reward isn't worth the steep price you'll have to pay for it.

Better to make or break it on the spot, go to your next call with a clear head, unencumbered by false hope. When I walked out of a callback situation, I counted it as a loss, over and done with, on to the next.

In a one-call-close simple sale, callbacks are the antithesis of working smart.

Callbacks are strictly for the naïve.

30

Record Keeping

"It is the mark of a truly intelligent person to be moved by statistics."

George Bernard Shaw (1856-1950)

Keeping track of work records is imperative for a salesperson. They provide numbers and ratios that enlighten and motivate. I kept daily, weekly, monthly, and annual work records: calls, owners approached, successful approaches (appointments set), presentations, sales, dollar volume, and commissions. Charts one through four are typical of the last ten years of my career, when I made 99% of my calls on Monday and 99% of my presentations on Tuesday and Wednesday. Occasionally I gave a Monday afternoon presentation.

An average Monday work-record sheet would look like Chart 1; a Tuesday or Wednesday sheet Chart 2; a weekly sheet Chart 3; and a monthly sheet Chart 4.

Chart 1 Daily (Monday)	
Calls	𝍸 𝍸 𝍸 𝍸 𝍸 𝍸 𝍸 𝍸 𝍸 𝍸 𝍸 𝍸 𝍸 𝍸 𝍸 𝍸 𝍸 𝍸
Owners	𝍸 𝍸 𝍸 𝍸 𝍸 𝍸
Appointments	𝍸 III
Presentations	
Sales	
Dollar Volume	
Commissions	

Chart 2 Daily (Tuesday/Wednesday)	
Calls	
Owners	
Appointments	
Presentations	IIII
Sales	II
Dollar Volume	$4,500
Commissions	$2,250

Chart 3 Weekly	
Calls	90
Owners	30
Appointments	8
Presentations	7
Sales	4
Dollar Volume	$9,000
Commissions	$4,500

Chart 4 Monthly	
Calls	360
Owners	120
Appointments	32
Presentations	30
Sales	18
Dollar Volume	$38,000
Commissions	$19,000

A salesperson was paid a 35% commission of dollar volume; I owned the business so I did a bit better—50%— plus, of course, all the profits the company earned.

Numbers Tell a Story

Let's take the monthly totals and see what they tell us. If you divide 360 calls into $38,000, each call was worth $105.56 to the company, $52.78 in commissions; each owner $316.67 to the company, $158.34 in commissions; each appointment $1,187.50 to the company, $593.75 in commissions; each presentation $1,266.67 to the company, $633.34 in commissions; and each sale $2,111.11 to the company, $1,055.56 in commissions.

Wow! Every time I dialed the telephone I earned $52.78. Do you think having that specific dollop of information motivated me to enthusiastically keep dialing away?

Does Old Faithful spout regularly in Yellowstone?

Each appointment paid $593.75; if it was after 4:00 p.m. on Monday and I had one more appointment slot to fill, do you think an extra $593.75 motivated me to keep on dialing until I filled it? As my grandfather Jake used to say, "You're darn tootin'!"

Don't Be Shortsighted

I've known a number of salespeople who thought it a pain in the butt to continually interrupt their work to mark work sheets. Obviously I disagree; I think they're being shortsighted. The motivation factor alone is enough to do it (I was always trying to top my best week in the field, which wound up being $26,750.00 in a short two-day week, in 2006). So is the competitive factor amongst salespeople within a company. If one salesperson is earning $52.78 per call and another only $37.82, perhaps it would behoove the second salesperson to spend time watching and learning from the first.

Knowledge is power.

Record keeping provides invaluable knowledge.

Create work record sheets, mark them accordingly; amaze yourself with the value of each call you make, motivate yourself with the value of every presentation you give, try to keep topping your best week, month, or year.

It works for the Pros and it'll work for you.

31

Make Sure the Customer Remembers You

"Youth, beauty, graceful action, seldom fail; but common interest always will prevail."

John Dryden (1631-1700)

If a prospect buys from you once, chances are good he'll buy from you again and again, especially if you make a lasting impression. The best way to accomplish that is to identify his passions—baseball, fishing, golf, politics, travel, religion/spiritual, family, et cetera—and tell a related story.

I once called on a remodeling contractor, and as I scanned his office for telling clues (see Part IV, Chapter 36, "Telling Clues") I spotted an autographed baseball encased in glass on his desk; the signature on that prized possession was none other than that of New York Yankee centerfielder Mickey Mantle.

Normally I would have used that baseball to tune in with the prospect *before* the presentation, but he *said* he was running late and time was limited, which turned out to be a lot of hooey. When the presentation was over and I had his signed contract and check in my breast pocket, I steered the conversation to the autographed baseball.

"I'll bet you wouldn't trade that baseball for a thousand dollars."

"Try *ten*-thousand."

He was a huge Yankee fan and Mantle had signed that baseball when my prospect was a teenager.

Mr. Friedman and Bobby Richardson

"I have to tell you a story," I told him. "When I was a kid of 14 or 15 we lived on the North side of Chicago, West Rogers Park, and there was a man, Mr. Friedman—he ran Friedman's Delicatessen on Western Avenue—who had been in the Army with Bobby Richardson, the Yankees' second baseman. Whenever the Yankees came to town, Richardson would get a bunch of tickets for Mr. Friedman for a White Sox/Yankees game and Mr. Friedman would pile four or five kids from the neighborhood into his car and take us to the game—box seats, the best in the house. After the game we'd go around back to where the Yankees exited the clubhouse to board their bus; Richardson would greet us—he was such a nice guy, a real gentleman—shake our hands, and introduce us to some of his teammates. I met all of them: Moose Skowron; Whitey Ford; Yogi Berra; and Number 7 too, the Mighty Mick; and I have to tell you, it was an unbelievable thrill to meet all those Yankee greats."

My client was enthralled, intent on every word of the true story I was sharing with him. We must have talked another 20 minutes, trading stories back and forth. When I renewed that town, he signed up quicker than Mickey Mantle could run from home plate to first base.

Everyone loves a good story, especially if it relates to a personal interest. Tell a good story and you'll pierce the heart of your prospect. He'll be yours forever.

Thank-You Notes

Another way to make a lasting impression is to send a hand-written thank-you note; because it's done so rarely, you'll blow him away. You'll show him that he's special, and he'll forever remember your thoughtfulness.

Stay in Touch

Call every now and then just to touch base, see how things are going. You'll reinforce the positive feelings you established with your stories and thank-you note(s). If you take the time to call when, theoretically, you're not selling, you'll have an easier time selling more goods or services next time around.

Put yourself in place of the customer. What does it take to make a lasting impression on you?

A master salesperson takes the time to draw out the prospect's passions and relates by telling a good story.

He writes thank-you notes.

He stays in touch.

He makes sure the customer remembers him.

32
Never Take It Personally

"It's not personal, Sonny.
It's strictly business."
Michael Corleone in *The Godfather*

If you ask a non-salesperson why she says so adamantly that she wouldn't sell to earn her living, more than likely she'll say something like, "I couldn't deal with all that rejection." To a non-salesperson, a prospect's "no" is seen as a harsh *personal* repudiation, a direct assault on her sensitive ego, a humiliation. A master salesperson is apt to roll her eyes at such a comment. As I said in Chapter 19, "Cold Calling," it's only business; a master salesperson never feels personally rejected.

A Numbers Game

I never took "no" personally. I took *responsibility* for it, but never personally, even when I sensed a prospect didn't like me or something I said. No batter gets a hit every time up and no salesperson closes every prospect she approaches or presents to. Selling is a numbers game, a law-of-averages marathon. My father used to say, "You have to get the no's out of the way, in order to get to the yes's" That's what a salesperson does. I celebrated victories and got over defeats as quickly as I could, usually in minutes, and then it was on to the next. Yogi Berra, famous for saying, "It ain't over till it's over," just as easily could have added, "but when it's over, it's over."

It's a free country; everyone has a right to say no. To take it personally, to hang on to it for dear life, to keep replaying it over and over and *over* again is to surrender your power to someone *who isn't even a customer*. Why would you do that? What possible benefit can it bring you? If you go to your next presentation with that kind of excess baggage strangling your concentration, you're allowing a "no" to do *double* damage to you and your selling career.

Sacred Purpose

A salesperson must have skin as thick as a rhinoceros's because prospects can be downright insulting at times. It should go in one ear and out the other. You're there to make a sale, that's all that matters; indulge in anything peripheral to that sacred purpose and you're being self-destructive. I'll talk more about this in Part IV, Chapter 42, "Killer Instinct."

Never take it personally; it's only business.

When it's over, it's over.

On to the next.

33
Learn from Your Mistakes

"It's always helpful to learn from your mistakes because then your mistakes seem worthwhile."

Garry Marshall, *Wake Me When It's Funny*

To err is human; to make the same mistake twice is as foolish as bungee jumping on a fishing line.

Crazy Norman

Let me tell you the dumbest, most muddle-headed thing I ever said to a prospect. It was 1974 and I was presenting to Norman, the scariest prospect I ever encountered. The man wore a pistol on his hip and spoke to me like General George S. Patton addressing a lowly buck private. He was cold and nasty as they come. I'd been in the business four and a half years, in business for myself less than two, and still raw enough to be thrown off my horse by this strident fruitcake.

I can't for the life of me recall the exact words that led to my stupendous gaffe, but I do remember I was responding to his reason for not buying.

What did I say that was so amateurishly doltish? I said, "But that's silly." Where that embarrassing "rebuttal" came from I couldn't begin to tell you.

He turned fire-engine red as he blustered, "Silly? *Silly*? Why you ignorant *sonovabitch*," and enraged, grabbed my five-inch briefcase and *HEAVED* it like a shotput halfway across the store, scattering my sales kit all over Norman's establishment—telephone-book-covers, contracts, blue cards, price sheet, testimonial folder, and more. It looked like a tornado had torn through the place.

Dumbstruck

I couldn't believe what I'd just seen with my own eyes. It took a few seconds to process the shock, then bile boiled up my throat. I could've shot the bastard.

Only *he* was the one packing the gun!—snarling and glaring at me like he might pull it out and use me for target practice.

Discretion is the better part of valor, or so I've been told numerous times, so, heart pounding like a jackhammer, I turned my back on him, hurriedly gathered the strewn contents of my sales kit, shoved them back into my battered briefcase, and with all the haste of a starving cheetah—*without another word* to that crazy lunatic—got the hell out of there!

Two Mistakes for the Price of One

I have to admit, it took more than a few minutes to get over that one; I'm embarrassed to say I had Crazy Norman's "dialogue"—to say nothing of my flying briefcase—banging around my brain for a few *days*. Two mistakes for the price of one.

You'll be glad to know I never used that "silly rebuttal" (pun intended) again.

No indeed.

We all make mistakes; you're going to make some, too. Perhaps even a real doozy like mine. James Joyce said, "Mistakes are the portals of discovery." Learn from your mistakes so you don't make the even *bigger* mistake of repeating it.

When you screw up, cut yourself some slack, but don't make the same mistake twice.

PART IV

SALESMANSHIP

34

The Approach

"There is only one way...to get anybody to do anything. And that is by making the other person want to do it."

Dale Carnegie (1888-1955)

I believe in a memorized approach. I used the same one for 38 years because, pure and simple, it worked. Not by itself, of course; without the ability to *quickly* rebut and arouse interest when a prospect politely, or otherwise, attempts to get rid of you, even a transcendent approach won't get you far. Think of the approach as a Christmas tree and the rebuttals (interest arousers) as ornaments decorating the tree; without the ornaments, all you'd be left with is a drab, barren evergreen.

Winging it

Salespeople refer to a non-memorized approach or presentation as "winging it." Some salespeople believe they're talented enough to just wing it; good for them. I'm recommending what I know works; winging it is what I did when forced to get off track, but having a track to get back to was always a plus.

Your company may have a scripted approach for you; if not, take the initiative to create one that's suitable for your business.

Joe Smith's Approach

Let's create a scripted approach for Joe Smith; Joe also sells advertising to small businesses, but you can easily adapt his approach to your business. On this call to an insurance agency, he knows the prospect's name: Max Jones; but that won't always be the case. Is it easier when you know the prospect's name?

Indubitably. If someone calls and asks specifically for *you*, aren't you apt to be more open-minded than if he says something like, "Is the owner in?"?

The receptionist answers the phone, "Jones and Jones Insurance."

"Max Jones, please."

"Who's calling?"

"Joe Smith."

"Is Mr. Jones expecting your call?"

"No, but I've been asked to call on him; may I speak to him please?" Joe speaks with strength and confidence.

"One moment please…"

Thirty seconds later: "Max Jones here."

"Mr. Jones, my name is Joe Smith and my company is XYZ Marketing. We do business with, oh, two- to three-thousand insurance agencies around the country and practically to a business they've told us we've increased their profits tremendously.

"What we've got is kind of a new idea in the field of business promotion. It takes a very short time to show our program, but if you're like most of the businesspeople we've talked to in Fresno, I think we can show you something you'd really like—

"—but let me ask you this: If at the end of ten, twelve minutes, I was showing you something you didn't agree with, I'm sure you wouldn't hesitate to ask me to stop—true?"

(Get an agreement.)

"I'll turn that around; if I could show you something good, profitable, something you liked, is there anyone besides yourself—wife, partner, business associate—who should also see it, or are you the *sole* decision maker for the company?"

"No, I make the decisions around here."

"Okay, what's the best time for you, first thing in the morning or later on in the day?" Always use an alternate of choice close; never ask an open-ended question that can be answered "no." At times I did it this way: 'I have an opening at 8:00 a.m. or right after lunch; which do you prefer?'

"I'm here at 6:00 a.m."

"That's a bit early for me; how about 8:00 a.m.?"

"Sounds good."

"I go by Joe; may I call you Max?"

"Sure, we're not formal around here."

"Max, would you do me a huge favor? I'll be coming from one heck of a distance tomorrow; if you'd block that on your schedule, I'd sure appreciate it."

"I'm doing that right now."

"Max, I'll see you tomorrow morning at eight o'clock sharp. I'll look forward to it"

That was pretty easy, wasn't it? However, most successful approaches don't go quite so smoothly; more often than not you'll have to use your rebutting skills to secure an appointment, and the need to rebut can come at any point in the approach—not all prospects will allow you to speak uninterrupted from start to finish.

Let's try it again; we'll pick it up right after we qualified him as the sole decision maker. Qualifying is absolutely vital; in a one-call-close you never give a presentation unless *all* decision makers are present.

"Okay, what's the best time for you, first thing in the morning or later on in the day?"

"What's this all about?"

"It's a marketing program I want to show you; our clients—"

"—I'm not interested; I've got all the advertising I need."

"Tell me something, your advertising, are you pleased with all of it?" I guarantee you, no businessman is pleased with all his advertising. Create a question for your business that points out a problem the prospect deals with and would jump through ten hoops to solve.

"Well…no…."

"Let me ask you this, then: if I could show you something you yourself really thought would work *far* more effectively than what you're *not* happy with now, would you at *least* be open-minded enough to spend, ten, twelve minutes to take a quick look at it?"

"I'm not interested in spending any more money right now. Things are tight."

"You just gave me the reason why I should show you the program; good marketing doesn't cost money, good marketing makes money. If you'll look at it with an open mind, I think you'll be glad you did, and if at any point I don't make sense to you, I'll shut up and shake your hand; is that fair enough?" Asking a prospect to be open-minded will work no matter what business you're in; so will telling him you'll shut up and shake his hand at any point if you don't make sense to him.

"Well…"

"—I can be free at 8:00 a.m. or right after lunch; which do you prefer?"

"Morning's best for me…"

That was a bit more difficult for Joe, but no matter, he got his appointment.

Typical Objections

Here are a few more objections you're likely to encounter, and rebuttals to neutralize them. Adapt them to fit your business.

(1) "I'm too busy to listen to any salesperson right now."

"I'm sure you're far too busy to waste your precious time, but let me ask you, as busy as you are, would you invest a few minutes if you knew for a *certainty* that what you were going to hear would produce *thousands* of dollars in additional profit?"

"That's a trick question; who wouldn't say yes to that?"

"Give me the opportunity to show you what our insurance clients rave to us about. You won't regret it." (Close by giving him a choice of times.)

This also was one of my favorite rebuttals to the "I'm too busy" objection:

"I know you get 20 calls a day and probably want to get rid of 19½ out of 20, but if you'll look at this with an open mind, and you're like most of the businesspeople we've talked to in Fresno, you'll be glad you did." (Close by giving him a choice of times.)

(2) "What's so special about *your* program?"

"That's what I want to show you; share a few minutes with me, Mr. Jones, you won't regret it." (Close by giving him a choice of times.)

(3) "I'm not interested!"

"No, of course not, you haven't seen the program yet. [This must be delivered gently, humorously.] Tell me, though: would you be interested in something if you *knew* it was going to be highly profitable, make a *huge* difference?"

"Of course, who wouldn't?"

"Let me show you why our insurance clients rave to us. We're going to have one of the top insurance agencies in Fresno on our program; even if you decide it isn't for you, at the very least you'll know what the competition is using to grab market share." (Close by giving him a choice of times.) Here we just threw a little fear of loss into the equation.

Another tack I took when a prospect said he wasn't interested was to tell the following story:

"My father has a cartoon framed and hanging on the wall behind his desk. It's a scene from an ancient battlefield, around the time they fought with swords, bows and arrows, and catapults. The commander is in his tent talking to his underling. The underling tells him that there's a salesman outside who has called on him. The commander says, 'I'm not interested in seeing any salesman! I'm preparing for the battle!' Do you know what the salesman wants to show the commander?—a *Gatling* gun. The point is it never hurts to have an open mind, does it?" I usually got a chuckle *and* the appointment.

A Rebuttal for Every Objection

After you've been in the field for a while, you'll soon be familiar with the principal objections used to get rid of you. You must create and memorize an effective rebuttal to neutralize each one. There is a rebuttal for every objection, and you must be prepared to combat any objection you encounter. The alternative is surrender, which isn't a pleasant thought, is it? You didn't become a salesperson to accept defeat without a fight.

If your quiver of rebuttals is stocked to the brim, you'll get your fair share of appointments. Remember, selling is a numbers game: you don't have to win them all; you only have to fill up your work schedule.

First-Name Basis

I always worked on a first-name basis *after* I set up the appointment: "I go by Bob; may I call you by your first name?"

Rarely was I refused. Others disagree with me—they prefer to charge right in using a prospect's first name. I never was comfortable with that; to me it seemed disrespectful. At the other end of the spectrum, using a prospect's last name throughout the presentation puts you in a subservient position, so I don't recommend that. I discuss the importance of equality in an upcoming chapter.

Don't Give Up Your Thunder

The approach comes before the presentation; they are separate and distinct entities. Your sole purpose in the approach is to set up an appointment to give a presentation. You offer the least information possible to accomplish that goal. You *never* give even part of the presentation while in the approach; give up your thunder in the approach and you've crippled your presentation before you utter the first word.

Delivery

Your delivery must be strong, confident, and enthusiastic. If you're not confident that what you have to offer is in the prospect's best interest, he isn't going to believe it either. You're calling on him to better his life; be excited about that and he will be too. And remember, if you're going to sell fearlessly, you must be his equal, not a groveling beggar (see Chapter 37, "The Importance of Equality").

You can't give a presentation without first succeeding in the approach.

Go make that call!

35

Setting the Stage

"A director is a choreographer, both politically and creatively."

William Shatner

A salesperson is to a sales presentation what a director is to a movie or stage production. Here's the ideal stage setting for a sales presentation: you and the prospect(s) isolated in an inner sanctum: an office; a conference room; in a residence, the dining room. You want comfort, control, and privacy; and each time you present, it's your responsibility to set the stage to maximize those three factors.

What You Don't Want

You don't want:

(1) an employee in the room who's not "officially" listening to the presentation, but who nevertheless is and might blurt out a negative comment, which could kill the sale. Anyone you're not getting commitments from is a potential sale killer.

(2) A secretary or other employee constantly popping in and interrupting, grabbing the prospect's attention away from you and the presentation.

(3) The prospect accepting telephone calls, which also interrupt the flow of the presentation.

(4) Having to present in a public area—for example, a glass countertop in a jewelry store, surrounded by customers and employees who draw the prospect's attention away from you.

(5) Having to present on the hood of a contractor's truck, especially when it's cold or raining.
(6) Having to present on a pile of boxes in a warehouse or garage.
(7) Having to present in a restaurant, with a host of strangers staring at you.
(8) A prospect's friend dropping by for a visit and staying to listen to the presentation.

Comfort, Control, and Privacy

When I walked into a business and the owner greeted me, I had a standard line: "Is there someplace comfortable where we'd be out of the way of everything?" Four out of five times I was escorted to an ideal inner sanctum—comfortable and private so I could exercise maximum control of the presentation. One out of five times I had to tough it out in a less-than-ideal milieu, every now and then in *horrendous* circumstances: I once gave a presentation to a fence contractor while standing up in the back of his covered truck during a rain storm. Naturally my closing percentage was significantly higher when the stage was set in my favor.

Don't Be Shy

A salesperson can't be shy or reticent if he's going to set the stage to perfection. I often positioned prospects so I could control the delivery of the presentation. "Max, may I ask you to move around next to Sam; that way I won't be at a tennis match."

"If I can put you over here, Sam, and angle my material towards you this way, I'll be fine."

"Is there a light we could turn on? It's a bit dark in here and I want to make sure you can see okay."

The prospect decides to position himself halfway across the room: "Max, can I pull you in a little closer where I can show you this properly?"

Referring to a television or radio playing and pointing to my left ear: "I've got a tin ear on this side—it's a present from my Navy days; is it possible to turn that down a bit?" I never was refused; half the time they offered an apology as they turned it off.

When a prospect's friend dropped by to chat and he obviously wasn't leaving any time soon: "Sam, we present our program only to the principals or key employees of the company; would you like me to reschedule?" I never was challenged; in most cases the friend got the hint and left of his own accord.

There were times I had to present to five (or more) decision makers and had to line them up so all could view the flipchart and I could have eye contact with them. I must say, I never had a problem—everyone was always quite accommodating. I believe they respected me for having the gumption to ask. The control I established was a bonus that helped tremendously throughout the presentation and close. I'll talk more about control in Chapter 43, "Control."

Don't Be Afraid!

A salesperson *can*not *be fearful of the prospect or feel like an interloper*; after all, the salesperson is the prospect's guest and *most* people treat guests with a modicum of deference, don't they? Also, the salesperson must not think of himself as pushy when setting the stage; he's simply creating maximum efficiency to properly do his job—another reason he must be on equal footing with his prospect(s) (see Chapter 37, "The Importance of Equality").

If you can't be bothered to set the stage, if you think it's too minor a thing to concern yourself with, you're foolishly putting a 500-pound weight on your back. Be professional and smart—set the stage; do it every time you're about to give a presentation.

You won't win an Academy Award for best direction, but you'll be an award-winning salesperson.

And you'll make more money.

36
Telling Clues

"It's the little details that are vital.
Little things make big things happen."
John Wooden (1910-2010)

When I walked into a prospect's home or business, especially his office, I always did a quick 360-degree scan to see if I could spot any telling clues as to his character, personality, or interests—including religion or politics. Here's a short list a salesperson can tune in on to establish a strong rapport with his prospects: photographs of wife, children, grandchildren, hunting and fishing, race cars and other vehicles, boats, politicians, hobbies, golf, tennis, bowling, professional and college sports teams, famous historical figures, et cetera; Bible; plaques and awards; prized possessions; membership in clubs and organizations, such as the NRA; diplomas; business licenses; testimonial letters from customers.

White Sox Photograph

In the expansive office of a Colorado automobile dealer, in a wall unit behind his desk, the man had a team photograph of the 1959 pennant-winning Chicago White Sox. This was in the early 1980s, long before they won the World Series in 2005. The dealer was about my age.

The second I spotted that photograph I said, "You're a Sox fan?"

"Lifelong diehard."

"Are you from Chicago originally?"

"No, but Dad's family was; my father, God rest his soul, was pissed to the day he died that Shoeless Joe Jackson wasn't in the Hall of Fame."

That led to a discussion about former White Sox players. I told him that Jungle Jim Rivera, right fielder on the '59 team, and my father were good friends. Rivera had a restaurant, Captain's Cabin, on Crooked Lake near Angola, Indiana; my father had a cabin nearby on Lake George. When Rivera went on vacation my father ran the place for him. I also told him the Mr. Friedman/Bobby Richardson story. We both had a ball talking about *our* team. (Today I'm a Cubs fan with seats at Wrigley Field; it would take a chapter unto itself to tell how that came about, but it wouldn't belong in a book about selling.)

I pointed to the photograph and said, "I think I can name most of the guys on the '59 team without looking at that photograph."

He grinned, said, "Go for it."

I not only named them all, I named them by position; I even named a few who hadn't made the World Series roster against the Los Angeles Dodgers.

My prospect was completely bowled over. We talked about Luis Aparicio, Nellie Fox, Early Wynn—all in the Hall of Fame now—and a host of others. "They were called the Hitless Wonders," I told him; "they won 35 games by one run—many of them 1-0, 2-1, or 3-2. Their idea of scoring a run was a walk, steal second, a ground ball to the right-side of the infield to advance the runner to third, and then a sacrifice fly to bring him home."

A Mere Formality

The presentation was a mere formality after that; that man could have despised telephone-book-covers and *still* he would have bought from me.

Tuning in to your prospect won't always lead to a sale, but I guarantee it'll increase your closing percentage.

Stay Alert

Never enter a prospect's domain without scanning his desk, other furniture, and walls for telling clues—clues you can steer a conversation towards to create a bond between you. A prospect that has something in common with you is easier to sell—his wariness has been diluted like a watered-down scotch.

Most salespeople are oblivious to this bonanza of selling power. A pity really.

If gold nuggets were raining down, would you scamper around picking them up or leave them laying there? If you don't scan for telling clues, you're leaving precious gold for others to seize.

Be smart, scan for telling clues and use them to tune in to your prospects.

You'll be amply rewarded.

37

The Importance of Equality

"Once the game is over, the king and the pawn go back in the same box."

Italian Proverb

To be successful a salesperson must have the prospect's respect and be seen as his equal. You're not a toy for his amusement; he's not a cat and you're not a ball of yarn. Most people are decent, and they'll treat you with a modicum of respect; however, occasionally you'll run into an egotistical wiseacre who will amuse himself by putting you in your "proper place."

Captain Bly

Crazy Norman was not the only nutcase I ever called on. In 1973 I sat down with an automobile dealer who the prior week had taken over a dealership in Ohio. This man's ego was the size of Mount Rushmore; he was brusque and dogmatic—a 20th-century Captain Bly. He wanted me to know he was God and I was a lowly fly he could swat at will. Before I had a chance to open my mouth, he glared at me and said, "I'll listen to your spiel for as long as it amuses me, but if I deem what you say dumb and ignorant, I'll personally throw you out of here on your ass."

I was in shock; no one had ever spoken to me so harshly (I hadn't met Norman yet). In one sentence the ass kicked my legs out from under me. It took a few seconds to gather my wits and respond. Part of me wanted to tell him I didn't do business with horses' asses and stroll out of there à la Bette Davis; but I was so angry I wanted this jerk's scalp hanging proudly from my sales belt. And I was going to do my utmost to make that happen, even though

I knew it was a long shot at best. Before I began presenting, though, I knew I had to regain some semblance of control, try to put the bastard in *his* proper place.

Navy Seal Training

I leaned in closer, placed both hands flat on his desk, and cold as dry ice said, "I'll stop whenever you want me to; I give that courtesy to everyone, but when I leave it'll be under my own power and you won't be anywhere near me, if you catch my drift? Unless of course you'd like the benefit of some private Navy Seal training." Notice I did *not* tell him I'd been a Navy Seal; I spent the majority of my Naval service punching a typewriter in Imperial Beach, California—Ream Field, HS-10, a helicopter anti-submarine-warfare squadron. The Seals would've wanted me like they would've wanted Peewee Herman. Nonetheless I thought it was a great bluff.

Seemingly amused, he sat back on his throne and waved at me to begin. He begrudgingly gave an inch of respect, but wouldn't surrender half an inch of control; I could see that in his wicked smile (okay, so maybe it wasn't such a great bluff). It was a minor miracle that I made it all the way to the close with this character, but I couldn't sell him; which probably was for the best, my anger notwithstanding.

You Can't Be Intimidated

When you run into someone that nasty, you've run into a force to be reckoned with, to be sure, but you must not be intimidated. If you are, you're deader than a railroad tie before you begin. A prospect will sense your fear like a dog, and once he does, *look out*, he'll chew on you like you're his favorite bone. You'll be his sport for the day. If you don't have a prospect's respect, the odds of closing the sale are practically nil.

I left that automobile dealer with the same refrain I did after suffering a loss to anyone I disliked intensely: "If you see one of our covers after the mailing, ask the automobile dealer on it how well it did for him; I think you'll be surprised, if not shocked." As my mother would have said, you're not the only fish in the sea, pal.

Presenting to Donald Trump

Barry Thalden once told me a great story about presenting to Donald Trump: "I managed to arrange a meeting with Donald Trump. We met in what later became the infamous Board Room on his TV show *The Apprentice*. My presentation was on slides. As I started to set up my projector, he immediately objected. Undaunted, I told him it would only take a few minutes and would fully explain the opportunity I'd come to show him. Once the presentation began he interrupted me several times, trying to rush me along; each time I told him I was just getting to the part he wanted to know about. I'd come all the way to New York to see him; I was going to do it my way, come hell or high water. I wasn't going to chicken out, be intimidated because he was Donald Trump. When the presentation was over he said, 'I can't believe you got me to sit through your entire presentation—my rule for meetings is 12 minutes and out.' As you know, I got the job." If Thalden can stand his ground with an egomaniac like Trump, you can do the same with anyone—*if*, like Thalden, you're fearless.

Equality Begets Respect

If you want a prospect to respect you, you can't be afraid of him. He puts his pants on one leg at a time, just like you do. He sits down on the toilet the same way you do. He's just another human being, not a deity; he has no power over you except to say no, and if he exercises that power, so what? In the overall scheme of things, his "no" is meaningless: you knew going in that you weren't going to sell them all. The losses don't matter, right? *Only* the victories count. You have to get the no's out of the way to get to the yes's.

You're there to serve the prospect, better his life; your best chance to accomplish that goal is to be his equal, not his doormat.

The premises may belong to him, but your dignity belongs to you and it's not for sale.

38
Enthusiasm

"Enthusiasm is the most important thing in life."
Tennessee Williams (1911-1983)

"You never can be too enthusiastic" is an axiom of selling; conversely, not being enthusiastic enough will cost you more sales than anything else. You can have all the bases covered—strong mental attitude, excellent work habits, salesmanship second to none—but if you can't crank up genuine enthusiasm for what you're asking your prospect to spend her hard-earned money on, you're the equivalent of a baseball pitcher without a fastball. You're going to get clobbered.

The Man Who Trained Me

The man Trudeau assigned to train me was the personification of hypo-enthusiasm; we'll call him Rollie—I'd cut off a finger before I'd embarrass this sweetheart of a man. Rollie was short, thin, dark complected, and exceedingly soft-spoken. I spent four weeks in the field with him and observed about three-dozen presentations (in the evenings I memorized a 26-page presentation); he closed only three sales, two of which were renewals. It got to the point I wasn't *expecting* him to succeed. Weeks later, after I'd sold up a hurricane, Trudeau told me he'd been worried that Rollie's lack of success would negatively influence me to take a hike. The irony was, Rollie was a superb trainer.

No Pizzazz

He would have been a terrific salesman, too, if only he could have raised his voice a few decibels and shown a little pizzazz. He just couldn't do it. Months later I was managing *him* and tried everything under the stars to get him to breathe a little fire, show some excitement. We drilled together for hours. His effort was Herculean—he tried and tried and then tried some more—he just couldn't do it.

Shakespearean Tragedy

I felt so bad for him. Selling was his choice of profession, a profession he loved and was knowledgeable about, but he was a freshwater fish swimming in the sea. It was a personality issue—just one of those ironic jokes God plays on human beings. Since he'd been in the business for a number of years before I showed up, he'd achieved some level of success; but for the life of me, I can't imagine how. Harry F. Banks said, "A salesman minus enthusiasm is just a clerk."

Theater

A sales presentation is a form of theater; a salesperson is like an actor putting on a performance for his audience. If he can't get excited about his product or service, the performance is a flop. The prospect will walk out before the second act. A prospect buys on emotion far more than on logic or reason, and if a salesperson isn't excited, the prospect won't be either; and if the prospect isn't excited—ho hum—*he isn't going to buy.*

You Can't Be Too Enthusiastic

I've seen sales made on enthusiasm alone, the prospect so bowled over by the salesperson's pure raw energy that he was signing a contract before he knew what was happening. I'm not talking about a phony televangelist staging a gyrating revival à la *Elmer Gantry*; I'm talking about a dignified master salesperson who's so enthusiastic he practically lifts you off the ground—you feel like you're participating in a magic show, but just can't comprehend how he's doing it.

You want to be a master salesperson?

Get excited!

And don't worry about being *too* excited. There is no such thing.

39
Visual Aids

"A picture's meaning can express ten thousand words."

Chinese Proverb

If you're lucky, a prospect will remember 20% of what he hears, but what he *sees* will stick in his mind like Velcro.

"Frankly my dear, I don't give a damn!" Think you would recognize that line from *Gone with the Wind* as clearly as you do if you didn't have that image frozen in time of Gable and Leigh on the staircase? Hardly.

Flipchart

I utilized a flipchart with 12 pages of bold type and artwork, arranged in juxtaposition to major points of my presentation, including each commitment I *had* to get to cutoff another possible objection. Each page was encased in a clear plastic sheath. I used a Cross® pen as a pointer to direct the prospect's eyes to the flipchart. If I had used an inexpensive throwaway pen or one with writing on it, I would have cheapened the presentation, which would have cheapened me in the eyes of the prospect. Every detail is that important; nothing should be left to chance.

Quite often a prospect asked if I needed an electrical outlet for a projector or other device. I laughed, told him I was a low-tech guy and that all I had was a flipchart. The point is, he was *expecting* some sort of visual aid from me.

Sunroom Salespeople

When Nicki and I built a sunroom off our kitchen, we interviewed three companies. All three salespeople used a flipchart or three-ring binder. The salesman from Champion (they built a sensational sunroom; thank you again, guys), Nate Greene, used an impressive glass-temperature demonstration to show the superiority of their glass; that, along with Champion's competitive pricing, helped Nate close us. The following year we replaced all our windows; Champion's quality craftsmanship and follow-up service earned that business, too.

Normally, a salesperson is at the mercy of his company regarding visual aids. I can't imagine a sales organization worth its salt not providing a well-thought-out visual aid; however, if you work for a shortsighted company, get your creative juices flowing. You'll do the company, your colleagues, and yourself a huge favor.

Visual aids—you'll sell a lot more with them than without.

And buy yourself a couple of quality pens.

40
Delivery

*"Acting isn't really a creative profession.
It's an interpretive one."*
Paul Newman (1925-2008)

In Chapter 34, "The Approach," I said, "I believe in a memorized approach." *If your business warrants it*, I also believe in a memorized presentation—what some disparagingly refer to as a "canned" presentation. (An example of a business that would *not* warrant it would be life insurance; a life-insurance salesperson must interview each prospect to acquire the *specific* information necessary to formulate a suitable plan; a "canned" presentation just wouldn't cut it.) I believe in memorizing a presentation because (1) it allowed me to deliver the same high-quality information every time I opened my briefcase; (2) it protected me from the often "fatal" malady "diarrhea of the mouth"; and (3) I never had to be concerned about what I said or when I said it. I had a track to follow, and when I got off track to rebut an objection or answer a question, I could get back on track and continue without any difficulty.

A salesperson who wings it will tell you he's not comfortable with a canned presentation; he thinks his prospects will be able to tell he's delivering a memorized script and will be put off by that. If he believes it, of course he's right. Remember, if you think you can, or if you think you can't, you're right.

I gave over 12,000 presentations and rarely did a prospect accuse me of making a canned presentation; on the contrary, I received hundreds of compliments about how glad they were *not* to be put through another "boring canned presentation." The reason for that was rooted in a script I *delivered* in a conversational manner, utilizing strategic pauses and even "mistakes" for effect, all of which created a winging-it-like-reality for the prospect. In other words, it came across as more off-the-cuff than the real thing.

Voice of Authority

Delivery is two-thirds of the presentation. A third-rate presentation delivered by a master is normally more effective than a transcendent presentation delivered by an amateur. Words without inflection, tone of voice, confidence, and enthusiasm are like calculus lectures: boring. Put them all together and you have the Voice of Authority.

When Al Pacino delivers his lines, can you tell they're memorized? Not if he's on top of his game. If you could, the story would cease to be entertaining. Is it an illusion? To a degree, but so what? What does it matter, as long as you're entertained? The same principle holds true for the prospect.

The type of business you're in and your company's presentation policy will determine if you're winging it or delivering a script. Either way, if you study and absorb the presentation well enough, a degree of roteness will come into play. The better you know the material, the better you'll perfect your delivery.

Adjusting Your Delivery

Tone of voice is something you must pay extra-close attention to. A master salesperson matches his tone of voice and language to his prospect. You don't speak to a prim and eloquent 60-year-old woman running a stationery store the same way you would address a boisterous 35-year-old plumbing contractor. To the eloquent woman you would say, "The rain in Spain falls mainly in the plain!" To the casual plumbing contractor you might put it, "Hey, the rain in Spain ain't fallin' anywhere but in the old plain!" You'd speak louder and more forcefully to the contractor than you would to the woman. You adjust your delivery to tune in to your prospect.

Confidence and Excitement

The confidence and enthusiasm of a salesperson are by far the most important aspects of the delivery. If your delivery is devoid of excitement, as Rollie's was, everything else is meaningless. Remember, selling is a form of theater; learn your lines and deliver them with aplomb.

41
Credibility

"Credibility is like virginity.
Once you lose it, you can never get it back."
Unknown

A prospect will not buy unless he deems you credible and trustworthy. Since he knows nothing about your character, and may believe *all* salespeople are lying bastards anyway, it's your responsibility to establish your credibility and trustworthiness beyond a shadow of a doubt. Prove you're the exception to his skeptical (cynical?) rule of thinking. This *must* be accomplished every time you present to a new prospect. But how do you prove yourself to a doubting Thomas while delivering a sales presentation? It's really quite easy, although, like all elements of selling, it requires due diligence.

Veracity

Always tell the truth; get caught lying and you're burnt toast—deservedly so.

Don't sell anything you believe is not in the prospect's best interest.

Don't promise anything you can't deliver; that's a lie, too.

Opportunity Knocks

If a prospect shows curiosity about a product or service you don't think is in his best interest, explain why you don't want to sell it to him. He'll be both surprised and grateful that you put his welfare above an extra commission, and he'll likely be your loyal customer forever or refer you to someone who will be. Whenever I discovered that a business was strictly commercial, I backed off immediately:

"I'd love to sell you our program, John, but it just wouldn't be in your best interest—we mail strictly to homeowners." Some of the strongest referrals I ever got came from non-clients I wouldn't sell to.

When a prospect asks for something beyond your power to deliver, be grateful because he's handed you a golden opportunity on a silver platter to establish credibility and trustworthiness. In no uncertain terms explain why you can't and *won't* do it. Don't be apologetic or fearful of his wrath—he's lucky to be dealing with such a straight shooter.

I often had a prospect ask me to guarantee him space on the front of the telephone-book-cover, and occasionally a specific *position* like the top-right corner. Since the ads were arranged in alphabetical order by business category, I couldn't do it; but instead of panicking over what I couldn't deliver, I grasped the opportunity to establish credibility. My response went something like this: "As you can see, Tom, all our ads are arranged alphabetically by category heading, so it would be impossible for me to guarantee you a specific spot on the cover; even I won't know who goes where until the last moment when the black-and-whites for silk-screening are put together. Also, real estate, for obvious reasons, is always on the backside of the cover. Not that that should bother you: our real estate clients, as well as other clients on the back, tell us being next to the calendars, community-information section, and personal-numbers section is right where they want to be. Also, because the books are laid both ways, there's equal exposure; it's a misconception that the front is better than the back."

I'd look him dead in the eye and say, "Finally, let me say this, Tom: I'm not about to promise you or anyone else something I can't deliver—that isn't how I do business." I'd treat that declaration like a closing question and shut up, challenging him to respond. A newfound respect was stamped all over his face.

A situation like that is akin to Ju-Jitsu: you take the force of the prospect's thrust and turn it around to your own advantage. There are similar opportunities in any business. Use them.

The "Easy" Way Is the Foolish Way

The company I worked for before going into business for myself used a cover designed so it could be put on the telephone book either way; there was no front or back. Our surveys showed the consumer disliked this screwy design because she never knew if she was grabbing the front or back of the book. The two-way cover was strictly a sales tool for a bunch of salesmen who wanted to solve a "problem." The irony is that it wasn't a problem; it was an opportunity to establish credibility. Often the "easy" way turns out to be the foolish way. Don't be afraid to take the challenging path to solve objections: confront them head-on.

Tuning in

Tuning in to a prospect's belief or interest creates credibility. He has a photograph of himself standing next to President Ronald Reagan: "Wow, you and Ronald Reagan; how did you get the opportunity to meet him?" That query led to a bond of commonality, which provided a ton of credibility.

You also can produce credibility by telling a personal story that implies the strength of your character. Let's say your prospect has been married 40 years and obviously adores his wife: "I've been married to my bride forever, too, Tom; I treasure her. I see how some of these Neanderthals treat their wives and I just don't get it; I don't see how you can call that love, especially the violent ones. Do you?" He'll agree with you and be glad he's dealing with a salesperson who sees life the same way he does. As long as you're sincere and speaking the truth, you're standing on high ground.

Voice of Authority

In the previous chapter, "Delivery," I spoke of the Voice of Authority. That by itself establishes credibility, trustworthiness. When Ronald Reagan said, "Government is the problem, not the solution" (never mind whether you agree with his premise), or "Mr. Gorbachev, tear down this wall!" he said it with such authority there wasn't a shred of doubt he was sincere and credible. Regardless whether you liked his politics, you had to admire his conviction and courage to speak his mind.

Look for opportunities to have your prospects see you in the same positive light.

They'll buy from you left and right.

42
Killer Instinct

"Now that I'm losing some, I can see how tough I was—the killer instinct, the single-mindedness, playing like a machine. Boy, that's what made me a champion."

Chris Evert

Killer instinct is the salesperson's unrelenting determination to close the sale. Her sole purpose is to accomplish that goal. That's how she makes her living and that's what she's there for. The prospect can be the blowhard jerk of the world, the worst hating bigot, personally insulting like Crazy Norman or the bully car dealer; the salesperson's white-hot killer instinct doesn't care: she's not there to judge, save, or convert him; she's there to *sell* him. She's there to put food on the table and pay the mortgage.

Cartoonist Bill Watterson said, "I'm interested in the issues but…I don't know…I guess I just don't have the killer instinct that I think makes a great political cartoonist."

Actor Liam Neeson said, "I was a boxer for nearly ten years, from age nine right up to seventeen, but truly, I didn't have the killer instinct. They said I was good but before every tournament I was the same, shit-scared. I'd be thinking, What am I doing here? Why am I doing this? What's it for?"

You must know what it's for.

Fighting for Milk

In Ron Howard's *Cinderella Man*, Russell Crowe portrayed James J. Braddock, a Depression-era prize fighter. Braddock's family has suffered terrible financial setbacks, and he's about to complete an amazing comeback by fighting Max Baer for the Heavyweight

Championship of the World. At a press conference a reporter asks what he's fighting for; nimble Braddock poignantly says, "I'm fighting for milk."

Stay Focused on the Prize

Let's say you're Turkish and you call on a Greek businessman. He doesn't have a clue what your ethnicity is but rants about 400 years of Turkish oppression—the blankety-blank Turks this and the blankety-blank Turks that—and suddenly your ears are burning red-hot, bile rising bitterly in your throat. The thought of telling him off and walking out on him is *so* tempting, but then you won't accomplish what you came after, and do you really want to blow the sale?

Or maybe you belong to Save the Seals and your prospect has a photograph on the wall of his buddies slaughtering baby seals. What do you do? How indomitable is your killer instinct now?

If you possess a mighty killer instinct, you'd rather swallow hemlock than blow the sale.

If I had a dollar for every time a prospect said, "I'm not trying to Jew you down, but…," I could take my wife to Hawaii. I find that slur offensive, but I always ignored it and continued to close the sale. I believe that was the correct non-action to take. No doubt a high-minded, "principled" critic would disagree with me, but it wouldn't change my mind: if principles are more important than providing for your family, knock yourself silly; I predict, however, you'll never be a master salesperson.

You're There to Sell

When a prospect cried poor mouth, said he couldn't afford my advertising program and then listed all his money woes, I had a choice: I could commiserate with him, "feel his pain," as President Clinton liked to say, put an arm around his shoulder, sympathetically say, "Gee, that's too bad, I'm so sorry; let me wish you the best and good luck to you—I hope next time I see you things are better."

Or I could look him dead in the eye and say, "May I ask you a question? Are you planning to remain in business?"

"Well…yeah…."

"You know, good marketing doesn't cost money; good marketing makes money. If things are as bad as you say they are, how can you afford *not* to have it?" That's a closing question so I'd shut up and let silence perform its magic. I was a salesman; I was there to sell; I was not there to be his priest, psychologist, or accountant. If I truly felt he didn't have the wherewithal to pay us, I'd walk, but "I can't afford it" is not an objection a salesperson with a true killer instinct pays any attention to. As the song goes, "It ain't necessarily so…"

In Sports, It's Mythical

Hall of Fame pitcher Early Wynn reportedly "would throw at his grandmother's head if she dug in too deeply." St. Louis Cardinals Hall of Famer Bob Gibson: "Step out of the box while he's in his windup and you'll eat a mouthful of dirt the next pitch."

In Chapter 10, "Motivation," I spoke of Michael Jordan's legendary competitive streak. Was there ever a killer instinct so deadly? Emulate Jordan's thirst for victory and you can't go wrong—with the caveat that you keep the prospect's welfare paramount.

Never forget why you're there: to make a sale. Anything that gets in the way of that laser purpose is a red herring.

43
Control

"A salesperson is to a sales presentation what a director is to a movie or theatrical production."
Robert Terson

Setting the stage is the first step to establish control of the presentation (see Chapter 35, "Setting the Stage"); being the prospect's equal is step two (see Chapter 37, "The Importance of Equality"). A salesperson can't be above or beneath the prospect in stature. If he talks down to the prospect, he'll be resented; if he subserviently begs for the sale, he'll be scorned. If he's to be respected and in control, he *must* be the prospect's equal, and his carriage and tone of voice (the Voice of Authority) must reflect that equality.

Commitments

A strong sales presentation requires commitments from the prospect in order to preempt certain objections that could pop up in the close; they also get him in the habit of saying yes and agreeing with you. The presentation I perfected over the years had numerous commitments; one went like this: "Does it make sense to you that many people in the area *can* be influenced?" If he disagreed, I had to retrace my steps to get a clear, unambiguous "yes." You must do the same.

"There's a reason Madison Avenue exists, Tom; they don't pay those guys the big bucks for nothing. Doesn't it make sense to you that good marketing works, that consumers *can* be influenced to do business with someone?"

"Well, yeah…."

If he mumbled agreement or silently nodded, I'd say, "Pardon…" or "I'm sorry, I couldn't hear you…"

"Yes!"

I got my commitment and I'd let him know I expected clear verbal responses. I was in control.

He's in a Hurry

A prospect will challenge you for control by rushing you along. He may repeatedly glance at his watch to signal his impatience, or say something like, "I didn't realize it was going to take so long; I don't have much time, can you hurry it along, give me the condensed version?" He may say he has another appointment, which may or may not be true.

"Tom, we do a professional program and we present it just as professionally. If I don't show you this properly and in its complete form, I'll do both of us an injustice and I won't have the opportunity to establish value with you. If you'll let me show you this properly, I think you'll be glad you did." Most of the time that took care of it; I diffused the challenge and remained in control.

Confrontation

A prospect is sitting across from you, arms folded across his chest in an "I'm from Missouri" pose and he's sneering contempt at you. What do you do?

You confront him, which goes against the grain for most salespeople because they're afraid of offending the prospect and the presentation ending in a lost sale then and there. It's the ostrich sticking his head into the sand. You're his equal, aren't you? You're fearless, right? I'd stop, look him dead in the eye and say, "You know, Tom, one out of every ten, twelve times I show this to someone, I'll get the feeling he's *so* leery that he's waiting for me to pull my machine gun out of my case and mow him down. I'm getting the vibe you're *really* leery and I want to tell you—"

I'd place my hand over my heart.

"—I didn't come here to throw a lot of garbage at you. That isn't my way." I'd shut up and give him a cold stare. The burden to explain his rudeness was his to struggle with.

Nine out of ten times (you can't win them all, remember?) he was embarrassed, apologized, and conjured up the best excuse he could think of. "Please continue," he'd say politely, his attentiveness and body language 180 degrees different. I had even more control now—proof that you must never run away from a confrontation when your instincts scream it's necessary.

Sometimes a prospect would go beyond icy body language and a sneer. He'd spit out what he thought of all salespeople, and it wasn't flowery poetry he was spouting: "You guys are all alike—all you want is my money and you really don't give a damn about me or my business. I can't stand any of you!"

It's useless to continue without confronting that cynical of an attitude. I'd speak in a quiet tone of voice, with a touch of justifiable indignation thrown in for good measure: "You know, Tom, there are still professional salespeople in this world who care plenty about their clients and do well by them. They make money for them, they protect them, they bring them great joy and happiness, they serve them with distinction and honor. I've always been real proud of what I do." Again, the burden was on the prospect to respond to the "whipping" he'd just been given. The typical result was total control.

Occasionally a prospect handed me an opportunity to establish an incredibly high degree of control even before I met him. I once had an appointment with a general contractor who was out on a jobsite. His secretary called on the two-way radio and said, "Charlie, there's a salesman here who says you have an appointment with him."

From the radio came his sarcastic response: "He's a damn liar—I don't have an appointment with him, he has an appointment with me." Pause. "Just tell him to cool his heels; I'll be there in about ten minutes."

When he arrived we sat down in his office. I immediately confronted him: "You know, Charlie, before I begin I should tell you—if you really believe I'm a liar, we're probably done before I begin showing you anything." I just stared at him. Red as a ripe tomato he stumbled all over himself apologizing, said, "I was just funnin'; please don't take offense, I really want to hear what you have to say; please go ahead, I'm all yours."

He certainly was.

Can you see the Ju-Jitsu effect?

If you're going to sell fearlessly, you must never run away from a needed confrontation.

Eye Contact

Another control issue is lack of eye contact. The prospect's eyes are the windows to his buying soul, and if you can't hold steady eye contact, you've got a huge problem. He'll stare at your visual aid, his feet, the wall—anywhere except you. What do you do? Since it's impossible for him to hear his name called out and not visually respond to who said it, I'd stick a hand out and call out his name, "Tom," and when he looked at me I'd continue. I'd do it as many times as necessary until he gave me the unrestricted eye contact I demanded. Control was mine, and it'll be yours if you use this technique.

Off on a Tangent

The most difficult control issue I experienced was a prospect going off on tangents, interrupting the flow of the presentation. It could be maddening. I had to be patient and listen attentively, but when it got out of hand I'd say something like, "That's fascinating, Tom, but let me get back to this so I don't burn up your entire morning; I know how busy you are and, believe me, so am I." Sometimes it worked and sometimes it didn't. There is no easy way to get a prospect who is running off at the mouth with unrelated stories to be quiet and just listen. Good luck with that. I wish I could offer a more effective solution, but…

The one who controls the presentation is usually the victor. Pay close attention to establishing and keeping control of the presentation. Don't be afraid of confrontations.

A master salesperson is fearless.

A master salesperson controls the presentation.

44

The Socratic Method

"Asking the right questions takes as much skill as giving the right answers."

Robert Half (1918-2001)

The more information a salesperson elicits from a prospect, the better his chances to close the sale. Fortunately, every prospect has a story to tell and is *dying* to tell it; unfortunately, most salespeople are in a rush to engage their mouths instead of their ears. If you take the time to search out what your prospect desires above all else, what his passion is, what his problems are, you'll be teed up for a hole in one; and isn't that a whole lot sweeter than a blind shot out of the rough?

Probing

Before you begin presenting, or later when you spot an opening, do a little digging. If Socrates had been a salesperson, here's a short list of probing statements and questions he would have found useful: "Tell me a little about yourself." "Tell me what makes (prospect's name) truly feel alive." "Everyone has a fascinating story to tell, what's yours?" "Everyone has a dream, what's yours?" "What do you want more than anything else in this world?" "What's the biggest problem you'd give almost anything to solve?" "How did you get into this business?" "What is *the* most important thing I need to know to be of service to you today?"

The brilliance of the Socratic method is that your prospect would much rather talk about himself than listen to you, and after he does you're going to pounce on those newly mined 24-karat-gold nuggets by performing an act of sales Ju-Jitsu, aren't you?

The Ex-Partner

Every so often a prospect would provide invaluable tidbits that led to a sale with a competitor of his. Some of those situations were downright comical.

In the early 1970s I called on a painting contractor at his home in northern Illinois. When I asked how he got into the business, I discovered he recently had lost his half of another company to a partner. He said the ex-partner had pulled a fast one and pushed him out. He was so angry that he spent more time talking about the ex-partner than about himself. By the time he was done I had a CIA dossier on the former partner and his company.

I wasn't able to close the sale. He desperately needed advertising but was flat broke, trying to make it on a shoestring and a prayer.

"I shouldn't've even started this company," he conceded. "I should've taken a job someplace for a while, got back on my feet; but I wanted to show that sonovabitch he was dead wrong about me, y'know? This would be perfect for me, but I gotta be honest with you—I don't even have enough to write you a check for the down payment. Maybe next time…if I'm still in business, which at this point is pretty iffy."

I sympathized with him. I could tell he wasn't blowing smoke, the man was sincere.

Twenty minutes later I contacted the ex-partner, set up an appointment, and went right over. Near the end of that presentation he casually mentioned the "divorce"—he was just as angry as the first guy—and I was off to the races.

"We know all about you and Mr. Jones."

He gave me an eyebrow-scrunching double take. "Oh really?"

I gave him a knowing smile; then proceeded to check off the lowdown his ex-partner had filled me in on. I thought the man was going to faint.

"My God," he gasped; "you weren't kidding, were you?"

"We like to stay on top of things," I said. Then I hit him with a serious dose of fear of loss: "In fact, Tim, Mr. Jones was one of the painting contractors on our list to call on, too."

"Over my dead body!" he spit out. "That space is mine! Write it up!"

And I hadn't even given him prices yet. I could hear Jackie Gleason whispering in my ear: "How sweet it is!"

The Socratic method is highly effective dealing with objections, too. Take note in Chapter 50, "Overcoming Objections."

Practice Makes Perfect

You can practice the Socratic method by using it in everyday social interaction. Let's say you're one of those conservatives who drive liberals bananas, and you find yourself in a discussion with one at a cocktail party; the two of you just met. The topic is capital punishment. Instead of shouting each other down (you know, both of you talking *at* each other simultaneously, neither listening to a word the other is saying), all you do is ask questions, no declarative opinions whatsoever; you just continuously ask him to support his viewpoint and see where it leads. It might go something like this:

Him: "Thank God there's been a moratorium on executions in some states; it's about time *somebody* put a halt to state-sponsored killing!"

You: "You're not alone in that opinion; I've heard others express the same viewpoint. Tell me why *you* feel the way you do about it."

"Well, I just think it's a good idea. The state shouldn't be in the business of killing people, I don't care how ghastly their crimes."

"Specifically, why do you think so?"

"It's an irrevocable sentence, man! There have just been too many damn instances of an innocent man sentenced to death; in Illinois it got to be a joke, there were so many cases."

"Do you see any possible problems with eliminating capital punishment?"

"Like what?" Sometimes the other guy inadvertently plays the game, too.

"I don't know; anything you can think of."

"Like taking away 'the deterrent effect'?" he sneers.

"You don't believe capital punishment is a deterrent?"

"No!"

"Why do you think others think it is?"

I'll stop here, but don't you. Take it far as you can. It's good practice for selling situations and you'll save yourself a lot of grief foolishly "debating" ("arguing" is more like it), which usually gets you both nothing but raw feelings and a headache.

Listening Attentively

After you ask a question, *listen carefully*. Absorb every word as though your life depended on it. Becoming a good listener is vital for a salesperson; it requires great dedication and lots of hard work. If you don't think so, why is it you can ask someone his name and *a minute later* you can't recall what it is? It's happened to all of us. Careful listening is so rare that it's become an anachronism.

Use the Socratic method. Keep asking questions until it becomes natural, habitual; and make a commitment to listen carefully, too.

The rewards for your efforts will be well worth it, I promise you.

45
Hot Buttons

"Hot Button: An emotional and usually controversial issue or concern that triggers immediate intense reaction."

Merriam-Webster Online

A hot button is a word, phrase, or story that instantly seizes a prospect's attention because it's specific to his business, desire, or interest. I did not include hot buttons in Chapter 34, "The Approach," because hot buttons are an element of selling and deserving of a separate chapter; but hot buttons are just as important in the approach as in the presentation—perhaps more so. No successful approach, no presentation.

Business Hot Buttons

An advertising salesperson quickly learns that every type of business has its hot button(s). The owner of a beauty salon doesn't care about getting any more business on Thursday, Friday, or Saturday; she has more than she can handle on those jam-packed days. But tell her you can bring in more business Monday, Tuesday, and Wednesday—her slow days of the week—and her ears perk up. Solve her most pressing problem? Please continue.

Joe Smith would tailor his approach to a beauty-salon owner by saying, "and practically to a business they've told us we've increased their profits tremendously, *especially on Monday, Tuesday, and Wednesday, the slower days of the week.*" In the presentation, he'd hammer the point home whenever he had the opportunity.

Before the Great Recession decimated the housing market, a real estate agent heard "listings" and became extra attentive; lately it's "buyers" that capture her attention. Mention "pre-need" to a funeral director and *she's* all ears. An automobile dealer wants to hear about selling more used cars—that's where she makes most of her profit. Talk to a florist about funeral and wedding business and you've struck the mother lode.

Personal Hot Buttons

My wife loves puttering around in the backyard. You'll often find Nicki in her vegetable garden or admiring the exquisite landscaping she helped design. The backyard is her baby, her prized domain. When Nate Greene, the sunroom salesman, discovered how important the proposed backyard landscaping was to Nicki—her hot button—he pressed it for all it was worth. He painted word pictures (see Chapter 47, "Stories and Word Pictures") depicting the joy she'd experience gazing out at the gorgeous landscaping while reading a book, eating dinner, entertaining friends and family, or just lounging around. It wasn't just the sunroom she'd love; it was the expansive *breathtaking* view of her prized flowers, trees, and shrubbery. Smart emotional selling, Nate (see Chapter 46, "Emotional Impact").

Imagine how many wide-screen televisions have been sold by zeroing in on a sports fan's hot button to watch his favorite teams in lifelike wide-screen HD-TV.

"But, honey," the wife says, "we really need a new dishwasher..."

"Yeah, yeah, I know, sweetie, but take a look at this baby," he replies, drooling over the 48-inch Sony Bravia®, imagining Cutler passing a 60-yard bomb to Hester that is so clear and sharp it seems like he's perched on the 50-yard-line at Soldiers Field. He isn't buying a TV; he's buying a "season ticket" to watch his beloved Bears.

When I told Nicki I was considering a Lexus SC430, she chortled and said, "You in a convertible? Please, it'll never happen—the wind would mess up your hair, darling, and that would never do, would it? C'mon, you're worse than a woman!" (This before Pete the barber sheared me like a sheep.)

Ouch! After 35 years she knows my hot buttons like Oscar Madison knew Felix Unger's in *The Odd Couple*.

Still, I had to go for a test-drive, and when I mentioned my beloved's "opinion" to the salesman at Arlington Lexus, Juan Estela, he laughed, said, "No problem, Bob," and proceeded to take me on Route 53 at 70-miles per hour with the top down to demonstrate that wind in *this* convertible wasn't an issue—not with the windows rolled up and the glass wind panel in back. Juan wasn't selling a car anymore; he was selling a convertible that wouldn't mess up my hair. To say nothing of the extraordinary pleasure I'd get showing my smarty-pants wife she wasn't so clever, after all.

Sold!

A hot button grabs a prospect's attention so you can create emotional impact, which is what we'll discuss next.

46
Emotional Impact

"The feeling is often the deeper truth, the opinion the more superficial one."
Augustus William Hare and Julius Charles Hare, *Guesses at Truth, by Two Brothers*, 1827

A prospect buys on emotion far more than reason or logic. Once you've discovered a prospect's hot button through the Socratic method, you can sell your product or service to that hot button to create maximum emotional impact—what Zig Ziglar called "Selling the sizzle, not the steak."

"DRAGON"

Remember Andy Pasek, the super-enthusiastic young salesman who sold Nicki and me our iPhones® and iPads®? When Andy discovered I was writing a book, he flashed a knowing grin as he clicked on a dictation app—"DRAGON." He dictated a short paragraph, tapped the screen once, and then proudly held it up for me to see that "DRAGON" had "magically" printed out exactly what he'd dictated.

"Think that might be useful to a writer?" he quipped.

Wow! I was constantly searching for my notepad and a pen when an idea struck; this was far superior. It was incredible. I was smitten. Nicki looked like she'd just seen a magician perform a magic trick. Andy didn't stop there, either; now that he knew my book was my hot button—my emotional-buying trigger—he showed me another half-dozen ways the iPhone could be useful to a writer. By relating it to my project, he truly made the iPhone sizzle for me. I wasn't buying a telephone; I was buying a bunch of writing tools, including a dictating machine.

Lifelong Dream

When I purchased my SC430, do you think I was buying basic transportation, or fulfilling a lifelong dream to drive a classy two-seater convertible? The first time Nicki drove it she looked at me with a glowing smile and said, "I feel expansive. That's a good word, isn't it—'expansive'?"

"Yeah, babe, that's the *perfect* word," I told her.

Travel Hot Button

I once called on a garage-door contractor who, when asked what he wanted more than anything else in the world, told me he and his wife loved to travel; it was their supreme passion in life. They desired to visit as many exotic destinations around the world as possible. From that point on I no longer was selling advertising; I was selling additional profit to pay for all the worldwide travel they were going to indulge in.

"Imagine visiting Agra and seeing the Taj Mahal. Or the Sphinx and Great Pyramids. Or being on safari in Kenya. Our clients tell us one of the great aspects of the program is not only the additional profit, but also the *extra time* that profit frees up so they can do more of what they want in life. Travel, for example. You're going to love what our program can do for you, Ted. Think I can get a postcard every now and then from wherever your travels take you?"

We hadn't gotten to the close yet, but he laughed, said, "Sure, you can count on it."

Emotional Jugular

Most salespeople will give a prospect every solid, logical reason they can come up with, instead of emotionally piercing his heart. But you're smarter than that, aren't you? You're going to leave logic for the logicians and go straight for the emotional jugular, aren't you?

You're going to think "sizzle," instead of "steak."

You're not going to sell a product or service—you're going to fulfill dreams.

Thus fulfilling your own.

47
Stories and Word Pictures

"To hell with facts! We need stories!"
Ken Kesey (1935-2001)

A salesperson is like a writer in the sense that she best delineates her story by using word pictures. She selects her words carefully because, like the writer, she's always searching for the referent so her prospect will see, hear, smell, taste, and touch the message being conveyed.

Searching for the Referent

Touch your nose; it's a referent for the word "nose." Are you wearing a watch? It's a referent for the words "watch" or "wristwatch." Are you sporting a tie? It's a referent for the word "tie." A referent for a word representing a tangible, like the above examples, is easy to grasp; you're probably not having any difficulty with it. But what if you had to come up with a referent for an abstract word like "anger"? As an exercise, stop reading for a few minutes and choose a referent for the word "anger." Remember, you must choose a word, phrase, or sentence which your audience can see, hear, smell, taste, or touch.

How did you do? Are you satisfied with your choice? Do you have a true referent for "anger," which any group of people could agree on? In a sales seminar I once asked 30 people to attempt this same exercise, also using "anger." Most picked other abstract words—"livid," "ire," "pissed off," "rage," "fury," "hard feelings," "enmity," and a slew of others, ignoring the principle of the five senses. A few managed to choose concrete examples, all right, albeit less than awe-inspiring. One woman said, "He smashed his fist into her face!" which personally I found quite disturbing, but this is a book about selling, not psychology.

The reason you see so much metaphor and simile in a novel is because the fiction writer is providing the referent for abstract words so you can follow the narrative through your five senses. The best example I ever read of pinpointing the referent for "anger" came from Mario Puzo's *The Godfather*. Early on, Puzo has one of his minor characters, the funeral director Amerigo Bonesara, in a courtroom seething (yes, "seething" is an abstract word) as the two young men who savagely beat and tried to rape his daughter (she's still in the hospital, her broken jaw all wired up) are given a three-year *suspended* sentence.

"He watched the happy parents cluster around their darling sons. Oh, they were all happy now."

To provide the referent for Bonesara's rage, Puzo said, "The black bile, sourly bitter, rose in his throat, overflowed through tightly clenched teeth." And, "Now his brain smoked with hatred."

My grandfather Jake loved the expression "*What* a country!" and used it all the time. If he was alive and commenting on Puzo's choice of words, he'd probably say, "*What* a referent!"

In "The Mound Road Story," I wrote, "Never in my life had I seen such poverty, not this up close. These were poor people, barely subsisting. In the tiny bedroom off to the left, there was a young boy and girl huddled together in a twin bed; they were staring wide-eyed at me through the open doorway. They reminded me of the cartoon characters in *Little Orphan Annie*. The entire shack could not have been more than 750 square feet; the dilapidated ink-stained sofa and mahogany rocker from Goodwill maybe. A smell of bacon hung in the air."

Can you see the shack? Can you feel the poverty?

Munching Popcorn

Here is a word picture created for a microwave oven salesperson. He's discovered his prospects—a husband and wife—love to munch popcorn when they go to the movies, which is quite often.

"You'll never have to go to a theater again, folks, if you want to enjoy delicious popcorn while you watch a movie. Just throw a bag of microwavable popcorn in, set the timer, and in a few seconds you'll hear those hot little kernels popping away like a string of firecrackers. Pour on a stick of hot melted butter, bring the bowl to the sofa with you, cuddle up and munch away—pure heaven. What with sky-high theater prices, my wife and I save a bundle now; and honestly, the popcorn we make at home in *our* microwave is a whole lot tastier than that theater stuff. They never put the right amount of butter on it, do they? You'll save a small fortune, too; enough to pay for the darn thing in no time at all and you'll enjoy your movies and popcorn in a lot more comfort. You're going to love it!"

Create a Word Picture

As an exercise, create three word pictures suitable to your own product or service.

Everyone loves a good story, and the best way to tell a story is by using word pictures. If you tell stories, and use word pictures within your stories, you'll be way ahead of the salesperson who just dishes out cold abstract facts.

Don't *just* be a salesperson; be a master-storyteller salesperson.

48

The Sixth Sense

"You must train your intuition—you must trust the small voice inside you which tells you exactly what to say, what to decide."

Ingrid Bergman (1915-1982)

In Chapter 3, "Are Salespeople Born or Made?" I said, "the born salesperson possesses an emotional 'radar detector'"; in Chapter 43, "Control," I spoke of confronting a prospect exhibiting negative body language and facial expression. The two points are intrinsically connected: if you don't possess the "radar," you won't be aware that a confrontation is necessary.

Think of this "radar" as the sixth sense, an omnipotent cognizance that tethers you to the prospect's emoting. You always know where you stand with him so, if necessary, you can challenge what you sense are storm clouds gathering on the horizon.

If you weren't born with the sixth sense, you'd better develop it; otherwise you'll never be more than a middle-of-the-pack also-ran. The great ones will run circles around you and leave you to eat beans while they dine on steak.

Remain on High Alert

You must focus on the prospect's body language, facial expression, eye contact or lack of eye contact, strength of commitments, and responses to trial closes—*and comprehend what emotions they represent so you can take appropriate action.*

You must do all this while simultaneously delivering your presentation—multitasking. This is where women have a decided edge, just ask my wife.

Rebel from Virginia

I once gave an abridged presentation to an elderly gentleman from Richmond, Virginia; it lasted all of five minutes. From the second I began he scowled at me like I was Jack the Ripper. When I confronted him, he said, "Ah jus' don't liike yaaankees." I told him, "Hey, I don't like the Yankees, either; I'm a White Sox fan." He wasn't amused, so I packed up and left—quite amused.

A salesperson without the sixth sense is driving blind.

Pay heed to the sixth sense, unless, of course, you don't mind being an also-ran.

49

The Power of Genuine Admiration

"You must be very subtle.... You have to treat a highly intelligent man as a highly intelligent man. You must make him immediately aware that you are taking him very seriously. And you must enhance his confidence. Flattery is simply to make a man believe he can solve his problems."

Henry Kissinger

Human beings are notoriously vain, which is why flattery is such an intoxicating elixir. Who doesn't fantasize about being praised, admired, or envied? We're all susceptible to flattery. However, let me warn you: if you attempt to beguile a prospect by flattery, you better sound sincere, or be prepared to have a fork stuck in you because you *definitely* will be done. Nothing will kill a presentation faster than a prospect's perception that the salesperson is a phony.

High-Wire Act

Praising, admiring, or envying a prospect is a high-wire act to be attempted only by a master salesperson who is 100% sure he can pull it off. His delivery is impeccably sincere and he uses a disclaimer first: "At the risk of sounding like I'm trying to flatter you, Jim..."

Genuine Admiration

If you climb up on that high wire, let me suggest you think of it as "genuine admiration," not "flattery."

You're in a prospect's private office, and behind his desk, on the wall, is a photograph of a 40-foot sailboat; it takes your breath away.

"Is that your sailboat, Larry?"

The prospect smiles, obviously proud of his toy. "It sure is. I take her out every chance I get."

"At the risk of sounding like I'm trying to flatter you, Larry…," [the disclaimer] "she's absolutely breathtaking. I've dreamed of having a boat like that all my life; I envy you."

He beams, tells you the story of how he came to buy his boat.

Your high-wire act is successful.

Let's try it again. This time the photograph on the wall is a family portrait of him, his wife, and two grown daughters, 20 and 24. All three women are exceedingly attractive.

You nod towards the photograph on the wall: "You and your wife have two daughters?"

"We do," he says proudly, "they're the love of my life."

"You're a lucky man, Larry. I'm not trying to flatter you, but all three of your women are absolutely beautiful. I can appreciate how you feel; my wife and three children—'children,' they're all grown—mean everything to me, too. I have two married sons whom I adore and one daughter, Jessi, who's supporting herself by working in a coffee shop and pet sitting while aspiring to be a playwright; I think she has what it takes to be another Tennessee Williams—I can't tell you how proud of her I am. I always tell people: every man should have at least one daughter."

The bond is established. He takes some time to tell you about *his* daughters' achievements. Again, your high-wire act is successful.

Genuine admiration in the hands of a Pro works; flattery from an amateur is a recipe for unmitigated disaster. If you tell a man his plain-looking wife is beautiful, a red flag will go up and he'll question the veracity of everything you've said. You've dug a hole you'll never climb out of.

Sincerity is the balancing pole that enables you to walk the high wire. Be sincere and you can't go wrong.

Fake it at your peril.

50
Overcoming Objections

"An objection is not a rejection;
it is simply a request for more information."

Bo Bennett

My father loved to talk about the subtleties of selling. As a child I looked up to him as a selling god and hungered to soak up his wisdom; I still was listening attentively at 66 when he died. It was like being Michael Corleone with the Don as my consigliere. He sold insurance, sewing machines, garbage disposals, cookware, wigs and other hair goods, and advertising. He was a warhorse and expert on the intricacies of selling.

Objections Are Buying Signals

"The man who gives you objections is not tough to sell," my father would say; "you can do a lot with that guy. The one who *doesn't* object, who sits there silently like a bump on a log, *that's* the guy you're gonna have trouble with. And the guy who tells you, 'Hey, you've got the greatest thing since sliced bread, I love it, I've never seen anything so terrific in my entire life…but I just don't want it,' and won't tell you why, *that* guy you can forget about altogether, because you're completely dead in the water with him."

Indeed. Objections are buying signals: the prospect who objects is displaying interest, which you can deftly rebut to your advantage—a selling-Ju-Jitsu move. He's helping you when he throws his objections at you.

The prospect who says nothing, gives you zilch to work with; there's little you can do except keep digging to find out what's on his mind. You may sell him, but you'll work like Annie Sullivan teaching Helen Keller, to do it.

The prospect who absolutely *loves* what you're selling but isn't buying and won't tell you why, as my father said, "That guy you can forget about altogether."

Don't Panic!

The key to objections is remaining confident, poised, and calm; not panicky, ready to cut your wrists because, oh my, he challenged you. The key to being confident, poised, and calm is your ability to refute *any* objection hurled at you, with a solid commonsense rebuttal. You internally jump for joy when you encounter a familiar objection—and after a while they'll all be familiar.

Rebutting

We'll rebut three basic objections any salesperson is bound to hear. Our salesperson sells windows and siding. Adapt these rebuttals to fit your business.

(1) "I can't afford it." He needs replacement windows throughout the entire house, but probably is loath to spend the money.

"Why do you think so, Joe?" 'I can't afford it' is ambiguous; we need to know specifically what he means by that, or if it's his *true* objection. Often a prospect won't divulge the real reason he's hesitant.

"Well, lately things have been pretty tight; I'm watching every penny."

He's sticking to affordability, but let's make sure it's his true objection. "In addition to that, Joe, isn't there something else in the back of your mind, another reason you're hesitant, something you haven't mentioned?" I learned this explorative query from Frank Bettger. It's a powerful tool to uncover a hidden objection; I used it all the time.

"No, I really like the windows; I just don't want to overextend myself financially."

Time to rebut, but first let's use an objection-limiting close to seal off any additional objections (see "Objection-Limiting Close" in Chapter 54, "Closing"). "If money wasn't an issue, Joe, would we have an agreement?"

"Definitely." He's committed to buy if we overcome the objection.

"I can understand your concern, but there'll never be a better time to replace those old, dilapidated windows, Joe, not with the government offering a tax credit. And you know prices are just gonna keep climbing higher and higher. You'll be way ahead of the game if you bite the bullet now instead of spending a fortune down the road, without the benefit of the tax credit, to boot. And think of all the money you'll save in energy costs. Besides, is any price too high for making your castle so much more beautiful? It's sort of like a Mastercard commercial, isn't it?—'priceless'! You'll be glad you spent the money now, Joe." (Shut up and wait for him to respond.)

(2) "I'll think it over and let you know."

"Help me out here, Joe; what is it you're not sure of? Is it the quality of the windows?"

"No, I think they're fine, as good as anything else I've checked out."

"Is it the price then?"

"No, the price is in line with the others."

"The terms work for you?"

"They're fine."

Placing your hand over your heart, looking like you're in a quandary: "Is it me, Joe? Am I the problem here?"

He looks aghast, sits upright: "No, no, I think you've done a fine job!"

"I'm lost, Joe. If the price and terms are all right, and you like the look and quality of the windows, and I'm not an issue, what's holding you back from taking advantage of our excellent offer?"

"Like I said, I just want to mull it over."

Time to rebut: "I know it's a fair amount of money, and like so many other customers you're anxious about spending it, but you'll never have a better opportunity to spend so little for so much, Joe. You can think about it for the next six months until you're as blue in the face as the Pacific Ocean and you'll never know more than you do right now. You're gonna have to bite the bullet sooner or later, and isn't it a good idea to take action now—be proactive—when everything is so fresh in your mind and I'm still here to answer any questions you have? Procrastination is for the fearful, Joe, and honestly, I don't think that's you. Now is the time to act. True?" (Shut up and wait for him to respond.)

(3) "Your windows are more expensive than the others I looked at."

"What others did you look at, Joe?"

"Brand X and brand Y."

"They're both adequate products" [never knock anyone, it's an axiom], "but our feedback has told us they don't measure up to ours, Joe. Many of our customers tell us they can't afford a Lexus, but they love having Lexus-quality windows beautifying their most prized possession, their home. When you consider how many *years* you'll enjoy the benefits of such high quality, the difference is really a pittance, isn't it? As Aldo Gucci said, 'The bitterness of poor quality is remembered long after the sweetness of low price has faded from memory.' [We haven't knocked the competition; we're just quoting Aldo Gucci.] If you'll do business with us, Joe, you'll be glad you did. Will you allow us to serve you?" (Shut up and wait for him to respond.)

Rebuttal Exercise

Each day for the next 30 days create a rebuttal for an objection you've encountered; don't skimp, be precise and thorough. At the end of 30 days your quiver of rebuttals will be well stocked. If 30 rebuttals doesn't cover every objection you've heard, continue until you possess a rebuttal for *every possible objection*. This exercise will produce thousands of dollars in additional income for you.

Third-Party Affirmation

Throughout *Selling Fearlessly* I've used third-party affirmation: "Our clients tell us…" The beauty of third-party affirmation is that your prospect can't challenge the claimants. They're not present to be challenged, are they? If instead you claimed, "I'm telling you, this is the finest window on the market, Joe!"—he could challenge you. Why give him that opportunity? Do you see the difference? Use third-party affirmations; they work and they'll save you a lot of grief and extra rebutting.

You'll Be Tested

Just because a prospect throws a lot of quibbling objections at you doesn't mean he's a horse's ass. Your prospect works hard for his money. He isn't going to spend it without testing you to make sure you're worthy to do business with. It doesn't matter how much he loves or desires what you're selling. There are people out there who think it's their *duty* to give you a tough time before spending their hard-earned money. They take pride in the flaming hoops they'll make you jump through to close the sale. You can turn that around to your advantage as I often did by "admiring" their sales toughness: "Joe, do you do this to everyone or is this just my lucky day?"

I got a lot of laughs with that "query." Often a wife, partner, or prospect himself, bursting with pride, would say, "No, he does it [I do it] to everybody." Sometimes they'd add, "Actually, I think he was kind of easy on you because I can tell he likes you." Objections ceased at that point.

Objections to a confident, poised, calm, fearless salesperson are keys to the treasure chest—an asset, not a liability.

Be happy when your prospect tosses objections at you; he's doing you a favor and facilitating the sale.

51
Reverse Direction

"People will buy anything that's one to a customer."
Sinclair Lewis (1885-1951)

In 1960, at the tender age of 16, I got a part-time job at Crawford's Department Store on Chicago's far north side; it was my second high school job. I cold called the store manager, Mr. Dickman (my parents bragged about my initiative for weeks), and he hired me on the spot to operate the price-tagging machine. A few months later I was selling in the Boys' Department.

Schmate

Twice a year Crawford's held their Dollar-Day sales. Additional merchandise was brought in, not all of it the same high quality Crawford's was known for. One Saturday morning before the doors opened, I was straightening a table of shirts and spotted one my mother would have called a *schmate* (Yiddish for rag): it was dreary beige and had ten thousand little brown tufts all over it (okay, I'm exaggerating slightly). It was uglier than a pimple oozing pus. I could not fathom *anyone* paying good money for that piece of *dreck*, let alone wear it in public, and I jokingly predicted to three colleagues (adults all) that no one would buy it. They disagreed.

Not only did someone buy that rag, two women reached for it simultaneously and fought for it like two starving hyenas battling over a zebra carcass. They both held on for dear life; it took the wisdom of King Solomon to settle the dispute. I remember thinking, Lucy and Ethel—Lucille Ball and Vivian Vance on *I Love Lucy*—would be hilarious portraying these two. That shirt could have achieved the folklore status of the chocolate candies gliding down the conveyer belt.

Would either of those women have been so desperate for that shirt if the other hadn't provided such fierce competition? I doubt it. Such is the power of something you can't have.

Take It Away

Reverse-direction is the salesperson's tool to "take away" the product or service from the prospect, or make him jump through a hoop to buy it. Its use is limited to certain products or services, but when applicable it's indeed a powerful sales tool.

I used it all the time. Let's set the stage. I'm presenting to a real estate agent:

"We're going to have only one real estate client on our program, Jerry, and if you don't want the space, it's certainly your prerogative to make that decision. I'll tell you this, though: if I had a dollar for every letter I've gotten post-mailing from a businessperson who regretted giving up *his* space to one of his toughest competitors, I could take my wife to China." I'd pick up the telephone-book cover and put it back in the envelope; in effect, taking it away from him. Then I'd hold up the envelope: "Are you absolutely sure you're willing to see someone else in your space, Jerry? It's up to you…"

Reverse to the Nth Degree

A competitive company sold their advertising on a totally reverse-direction basis. They used expressions like "if you qualify," "if you're approved," and "if you can get it." This is the height of reverse-direction and not something most salespeople can get away with.

Personally I didn't want to, but that's just me.

"Taking it away" from the prospect, though, is perfectly within the ethical rules of selling. If there's a way to incorporate reverse-direction in your presentation, go for it—it works.

Just think of those two women battling over that *ugly* shirt. People want what they can't have.

Take it away and watch them reach for it.

52
Testimonials

"Documents create a paper reality
we call proof."
Mason Cooley (1927-2002)

Testimonials provide demonstrative evidence to validate what the salesperson has asserted about his product or service—the proof sequence of the presentation. Testimonials are an absolute must. A presentation without testimonials is like a wad of cotton candy—sweet but devoid of fiber.

In my business we used four types of testimonials:

(1) **Blue reply cards** sent back by homeowners; every so often a client would send in a blue-reply-card testimonial. I had *stacks* of them to show a prospect.

(2) **Letters** from non-mailing-list homeowners requesting telephone-book covers, and letters from mailing-list homeowners requesting additional covers. I kept them in their original envelopes to show the return address and cancelled postmark.

(3) **Testimonial letters** from satisfied clients. I kept these encased in plastic sheaths in a three-ring binder and updated the binder every six months.

(4) **Letters** from non-clients requesting ad space in future mailings. These, too, were kept in their original envelopes.

I've included examples of each, but have omitted names and addresses for legal reasons. Since blue-reply-cards were my personal favorite form of proof, I've included 15, five each from Springfield, Missouri; Tallahassee, Florida; and Columbus, Georgia. I've added punctuation for clarity and combined paragraphs to save space; otherwise, the wording is exact.

Blue Reply Cards

Springfield, Missouri

(1) "There are some listings prominently displayed. It seems to make my phone book more 'official' & helps me to think of using it more."
(2) "No pages to open to find common and emergency numbers. Thanks! This works…like it."
(3) "I will refer to the cover first for needed services."
(4) "Wonderful. Glorious. Thank you."
(5) "Preserves pages. Points to locations. You can't buy it otherwise."

Tallahassee, Florida

(1) "They took the time and made an effort to 'advertise' their services. Hopefully they will prove to be reliable. Keeps things nice which is important and #s/ads on outside save me time. Thank you!!"
(2) "Front & back of commonly, frequently used phone book."
(3) "I can tuck other useful notes & #s into inside pockets. Not only does it have many handy phone #s, it keeps the telephone book protected & looks nice. Thank you!"
(4) "A couple of my favorite businesses are on the cover & there is room on the cover for me to write in a few other common numbers. It's a nice gift for me because it's a lot more durable than the paper cover."
(5) "Most numbers are on the cover front or back. It keeps the phone book in better condition plus numbers @ a glance."

Columbus, Georgia

(1) "Bold print. Clearly written! Easier to find in alphabetical order. Helpful numbers & easily read cover."
(2) "Having numbers I use @ fingertip. Being able to put #s I use on cover – easy access. Thank U."
(3) "Very well organized. Just simple and convenient."
(4) "Quick and easy. Avoids having to look up. Please continue these. High quality and useful."
(5) "It's right on the front cover. Very convenient. Protects my phone book and business phone numbers are featured right on the cover."

Blue-Reply-Card Testimonial

El Paso, Texas Locksmith

"I love you guys! Customers have already come into the shop thanking us for the covers. Had my doubts…not any more!"

Homeowner Letters

Eugene, Oregon

"Thank you for sending the phone book covers so quickly. They are a very high quality & fit perfectly. My old one was held together with tape so I threw it away! I hope you are able to get more of these out to the public."

Des Moines, Iowa

"Is it possible to get 2 or 3 telephone book covers? It keeps the phone book so nice. Happy New Year."

Wichita, Kansas

"We recently received a new Community Service cover for our telephone book. Please let us know if we can purchase two more covers. If so what is the cost for two covers? Thank you." (As always, the covers were sent free of charge.)

Kentwood, Michigan

"Hi! I received a phone book cover in the mail the other day & was telling my sister-in-law about it. She said she didn't get anything like it in the mail. I was wondering if you could possibly send me a couple extra ones for mother & her. By the way, I really like mine! Thanks!" The postscript read, "Have a Super day & thanks again."

Client Testimonial Letters

Stockton, California, Insurance Agency

"Now that the phone book covers have been distributed, I wanted to write and thank you for your services. We are getting calls already. As promised you delivered on time and your follow through was perfect to assure my happiness with your product. Again, thank you for your professional and courteous service."

Kalamazoo, Michigan, Funeral Home

This was my first testimonial letter after going into business for myself—I had it framed: "We are pleased with the recent distribution of phone book covers which you made in our area. The design and quality of the covers is excellent. We feel that this type of advertising is an important part of our advertising program."

Non-Client Request Letter

Germantowne, Tennessee, Insurance Agency

"The next time you are doing a telephone book cover, I would be interested in advertising for the Germantowne and/or Collierville, Tennessee, cover area. I have attached my business card for your convenience in contacting me."

Videotaped Testimonials

My friend Barry Thalden recently pointed out that in our modern technological world, videotaped testimonials from satisfied clients and consumers would be an even more powerful proof sequence than what I used for four decades. I concur, go for it. Despite my non-techie nature, if I were still selling advertising, I'd pounce on that idea quicker than Brian Urlacher can sack a quarterback.

Testimonials are an essential part of a sales presentation. I cannot imagine presenting without them, but if you're not, it's time to start.

You'll see a world of difference in your closing percentage.

53
Pitfalls to Avoid

"Mistakes, obviously, show us what needs improving. Without mistakes, how would we know what we had to work on?"

Peter McWilliams, *Life 101* (1949-2000)

A salesperson can make mistakes that short-circuit a prospect's attention and blow the sale, but be oblivious to what he's done and unable to put a finger on what went awry.

Overused Words or Phrases

Remember Rollie, the man who trained me? A word he used incessantly kept grabbing my attention to the point I started listening for it. The word was "candidly." He began almost every rebuttal with it. It was "candidly" this and "candidly" that. "Candidly, Sir, we…" When I mentioned it, he was stunned, he had no idea he was doing it.

"You Know"

Have you ever listened to an athlete interviewed on television? Their "candidly" is "you know." They all do it. It's difficult for them to go more than five seconds without tossing one in. "Yeah, Chris, I'm looking forward to getting back with the team, you know, I've missed all the action, you know, it'll be a relief to get back on that mound again, you know." As an exercise, watch three interviews and count how many times "you know" cuts into the flow of their speech. You'll be amazed—you know?

The lesson is, *listen to yourself.* If there's a "candidly" or "you know" in your repertoire, *get rid of it.* It's costing you money. Consider joining Toastmasters; they'll help you immensely.

Take Responsibility

Have you ever had someone say, "You're missing my point"? Does that irk you? I'll bet it does. Do salespeople say, "You're missing my point"? All the time. Do you think it annoys the prospect? Bet on it. When a prospect wasn't grasping my point, I took a different tack. I'd say, "I'm sorry, I'm not making myself clear; let me try again." I took *responsibility* for the lack of communication between us, which is where it belongs. It was my job to be clear, not his to listen more carefully. Besides, why needlessly irritate a prospect? This is not a minor issue, it can cost you plenty.

Win a Battle, Lose the War

Another huge mistake is to debate a meaningless point. What good is it to win a battle but lose the war? It's just plain dumb. If I felt I needed to disagree with a prospect, I'd preface my remarks with a disclaimer: "I don't want to win a battle and lose the war, John, but…" It softened my contradiction. Use it, it works.

Other Do's and Don'ts

Some of these were mentioned in Chapter 27, "Common Sense Basics," but are worth repeating:

Refresh Sales Kit Periodically

Don't ever present with frayed materials or a messy briefcase.

Qualify for Decision Makers

Always qualify for decision makers. Don't present unless all decision makers are there.

Punctuality

Be on time for appointments. Don't burn up another person's time; if being late is unavoidable, call, apologize, and explain; reschedule, if necessary.

Car Washes

Don't pull up to a prospect's place of business or home in a filthy automobile; get a car wash.

Personal Hygiene

Don't show up needing a shower, shave, deodorant, or in a wrinkled suit. If you get mustard on your tie at lunch, buy a new one.

Personal Problems

Don't share your personal troubles with a prospect; that's what bartenders are for.

Little things can kill a sale easily as the big ones. Listen to yourself; dot the i's and cross the t's.

Do you get it? I hope so; otherwise I didn't make myself clear, did I?

54
Closing

"Always be closing...That doesn't mean you're always closing the deal, but it does mean that you need to be always closing on the next step in the process."

Shane Gibson

The close is the finale of the presentation, but the closing *process* commences the instant the salesperson qualifies for decision makers. From that point on, the salesperson leads the prospect towards the close like a cowboy herds a steer towards the narrowest point of the corral, where the prospect's desire will be fulfilled.

Commitments

A well-constructed presentation has commitments you *must* elicit before you continue on. *You do not go forward until you get that commitment*, or it's possible you'll hear an objection on that point when you reach the close. Each commitment closes a door (the corral narrows) on the prospect. If he's agreed that advertising influences people, he "can't" object at the close that advertising doesn't work—theoretically, anyway. It isn't 100% foolproof, thus the quotation marks around "can't." Slippery prospects have been known to renege on a commitment.

Trial Closes

A trial close lets you know how you're doing with the prospect, whether you're making sense to him or not. Right after going through the proof sequences, I would ask, "Don, am I making sense to you?"

If he balked, I attempted to elicit his objections so I could deal with them right then and there. That's what you do when the prospect "isn't with you." *You do not move on to the close if any doors are still open.*

If he said yes, I'd move to a pre-price commitment: "If the price were right in *your* judgment; if *you* felt it was correct for the tremendous benefits provided, would you want to be our bicycle dealer here in Lexington?"

If he balked, see above.

If he affirmed, I took out a contract and pricing sheet (encased in a clear plastic sheath) and quoted each ad-size's price per home and total cost, and then went directly to a closing statement: "Size is up to you." *And then I'd shut up*!

The First One Who Talks Loses

It may be a cliché, but it's true: you do not utter a syllable after a closing statement or question. I don't care how long it takes, you look the prospect dead in the eye and *wait* for him to either: (1) give you a buying signal, (2) toss an objection (not a bad thing), (3) ask a question, (4) or say no. The heavy silence between you is your ally; it's pressure the prospect must deal with.

I once sat there 25 minutes with a car dealer, our eyes locked in frozen combat, the silence between us as thick as an iceberg. *Twenty-five minutes*! The man was testing me. He knew the salesperson's Closing Rule of Silence and was out to break me. I refused to give in. I said not a syllable, nor did I break eye contact with him. Finally a begrudging smile crept across his face; he exhaled, as though he'd been holding his breath the entire time. He threw his hands up in exasperation and said, "Man! You're the first guy I ever met who wouldn't give in." He snatched up the contract and said, "Let me look at this damn thing." That sale was sweet as Truman poking fun at the *Chicago Tribune* for their infamous headline gaffe after he defeated Dewey.

Again, the prospect's four choices are: (1) give a buying signal—perhaps a nod of the head and "Looks good to me, I do like it"; (2) toss an objection—"I'm not completely convinced, I'll think it over"; (3) ask a question—"When did you say the covers are going to be delivered?"; (4) or simply say, "No, I don't want it," or some other definitive form of "no" like "I think I'll pass." Once in a chartreuse sunset a prospect would point to a specific-size ad and say, "I'll take *that* one." It always caught me by surprise—it just seemed too easy.

Buying Signal

A buying signal calls for an immediate closing question, as your pen hovers over the contract: "What is the exact official name of the company?"

If he answers, fill out the contract. You want to be quick as Jeff Gordon flying out of a turn; the ideal timeframe is less than 30 seconds. Why give a nervous prospect an opening to change his mind? If you're smart, you'll drill until you meet the 30-second standard.

If he balks, stop, look surprised, and say, "Is there something you're not sure of?" At that point either you'll go back to writing up the contract, answer a question, or rebut an objection. If it's writing up the contract, fill it out, then turn it around so it's facing the prospect, "X" where he needs to sign, then firmly hand him your pen (he'll take it) and say, "I just need your okay right here." ("Sign" is not a word you want to use. Have him "okay" it for you. He's probably been warned a thousand times not to "sign" anything. Haven't you?)

Then shut up again!

The silence will be even thicker now, as he carefully examines the contract. Slowly, ever so slowly, he'll bring the pen to the "X" and sign it.

Objection

If the prospect throws an objection, simply rebut the objection (your quiver is chock full of rebuttals, right?), then make sure the rebuttal was successful: "Does that make sense to you, Don?"

Get a commitment.

"Yes."

Now swing right into the contract close: "What is the exact official name of the company?" (Shut up!)

Question

If the prospect asks a question, answer it; then confirm you answered it to his satisfaction: "Did I answer that satisfactorily for you, Don?"

"Yes."

If he's not satisfied with your answer, try again until he is. Then swing right into the contract close.

He Says No

If the prospect isn't buying, try, "I'm sure you're saying that for a good reason; may I ask why you feel that way?" You should get an objection; see above for how to proceed when getting an objection.

Don't forget to use the hidden objection query from Frank Bettger (see Chapter 50, "Overcoming Objections").

Closing Statements and Questions

Here are five closing statements and questions I used before swinging into a contract close, my favorite. Adapt them to fit your business:

"If you'll allow us to serve you, Don, you'll be glad you did." (Shut up!)

"I'll tell you this, we're going to make a lot of money for our bicycle dealer; you'll be glad you're the bicycle dealer in that space, and not someone else." (Shut up!)

"Will you allow us to serve you?" (Shut up!)

"Would you like to be listed under 'Bicycle Dealer' or 'Bicycles'?" (Shut up!)

"If you'll have a little faith, Don, I think that faith will be well rewarded." (Shut up!)

Closes

In my youth, I once heard the late J. Douglas Edwards, in his time often referred to as "the Father of Modern Selling," say that most salespeople knew two closes and used only one of them. He thought a good salesperson should know 50. Personally I think that's excessive, but who am I to disagree with "the Father of Modern Selling"?

Here are six closes I liked to use. Adapt them to fit your business or create your own to do the same:

"The Contract Close"—see above.

"The Artwork Close"—I enticed him into helping me create the ad.

"The Alternate of Choice Close"—"Would you like to be listed under 'Bicycle Dealer' or 'Bicycles'?"

"The Fear of Loss Close"—"You'll be glad you're in that space, Don, and not one of the other bicycle dealers referred to us. I've had people get a cover in the mail, with their toughest competitor in the space they turned down, and go absolutely bananas. If you'll try us once, you'll never give up that space."

"The Besides the Money Close"—"Besides the money we're going to make for you, Don, having your friends, neighbors, and customers ["clients" for businesses like insurance] tell you they saw you on the cover will be like a Mastercard commercial—'priceless.'"

"The Objection-Limiting Close"—"If I could do that for you, do you definitely want the space?" As opposed to jumping right to, "You've got it, Don!" You lead him to commit to buy, *if* you can satisfy his objection or request; otherwise plan on hearing another objection or, worse, a whole string of objections.

If you're ambitious enough to learn the 50 closes J. Douglas Edwards recommended, I suggest you pick up a copy of *Zig Ziglar's*

Secrets of Closing the Sale. It's the best book on closing I ever read and will help you become an expert closer. The amiable, humorous Ziglar will entertain you, as well as enlighten you.

The characteristics of a strong closer are identical to that of a strong presenter: enthusiasm; power of delivery (the Voice of Authority); quiver full of potent rebuttals; plus five to 15 effective closes and a score of closing statements and questions; *and the assumption that the prospect eventually is going to say "yes*."

Ask for the Order!

When my brother joined me in the advertising business, like so many other salespeople I've known, he was afraid to ask for the order. When Dad came into the field to work with him, they went back to the prospects Harlan thought he'd been close to selling but for some reason didn't close. The first thing Dad would say to the prospect was, "It would be a great help if you could tell us why you didn't buy our program." If the prospect had an objection, Dad delivered a rebuttal and a closing question, sometimes closing the sale. If the prospect couldn't come up with an answer, said, "You know, I really don't know why, I liked your program," he closed him on the spot. This occurred a number of times. My brother thought our father was performing magic; he wasn't, he was just asking for the order from someone who'd been sold, or partially sold, but not closed.

Don't be afraid to ask for the order. It's an axiom of selling fearlessly.

Don't give up too easily. I hung in there until I was 100% positive I wasn't going to make the sale—and then hung in there a bit longer.

Napoleon Hill said, "The most interesting thing about a postage stamp is the persistence with which it sticks to its job."

Hang in there!

55
Post-Closing

"The best way to knock the chip off your neighbor's shoulder is to pat him on the back."

Anonymous

A cancellation—buyer's remorse—will puncture a salesperson's balloon faster than warp speed in *Star Wars*. If it occurs when the salesperson is particularly vulnerable, it can be devastating; she's already celebrated the sale and chalked up the commission on the tote board, then *BOOM*, it's cruelly yanked away from her. She'd have been better off if the prospect said no to begin with; in fact, she wishes he had. She stares at the telephone and angrily contemplates heaving it out the window. She wracks her brain trying to solve the mystery of what went wrong—who or what killed this deal? For the next day or two when the telephone rings, she feels a stab of alarm—*Oh no, not another one*. Two cancellations in the same week and she's paranoid as Macbeth.

Horrendous Week

Let me tell you about one of the worst weeks I ever had in the field. To fully appreciate this story, you should know that opening a new town was stressful. I couldn't relax until I had that first sale under my belt.

It was late fall 1988; Monday morning, 6:00 a.m. and pitch black outside as I drove from Salt Lake City heading north on I-15 towards Spokane, Washington. Five miles north of the Utah/Idaho border a pair of glowing eyes darted across the road. Fascinated, I tracked the animal as it bounded up into the foothills. I thought it was a mountain lion.

It wasn't; it was a deer. When I looked back to the road the deer's mate was right on top of me—*CRASH*! I never had a chance; I *smashed* into her at 60 miles an hour, killing her instantly. My car was dead too; I managed to coast to the shoulder 50 feet beyond the carcass of that unlucky doe. (You would not believe all the Bambi-killer jokes I endured for the next six months.)

With the aid of a flashlight, I assessed the damage. The grill looked like a smashed-in accordion covered in deer fur and blood. Sick to my stomach, I got back into the car, gripped the steering wheel, and at the top of my lungs screamed a tirade of obscenities. I could have wept. I thought of the water gushing out from under the hood on Mound Road. Oh, this was so much worse. I could do nothing except shiver in the dark, pray, and wait for someone, anyone, to come by and help me. *Please*!

An hour later a man pulled over, picked me up, and drove me to the sheriff's office. As I sipped hot coffee and tried to warm up, the deputy told me how lucky I was: one out of four times the deer comes flying up the hood, crashes through the windshield, hooves kicking wildly, and wipes out the driver—as in d-e-a-d.

Phew!

Briefly, here's what happened next: I drove with the tow-truck driver north to Pocatello and dropped off the car at a body shop; made arrangements to have it delivered to Spokane when it was repaired; made arrangements to fly to Spokane; flew to Spokane the next morning, with just my traveling bag and briefcase; rented a car and got situated to work the town. I started making calls later that afternoon. I managed to give four presentations Wednesday, wrote two of them for a total of $3,500 worth of business. Nothing earth-shattering, but all things considered, I was overjoyed as Dorothy going back to Kansas and proud of myself: I'd kept my wits about me during a harrowing ordeal and still managed to open the town and write *some* business.

Buyer's Remorse

Within a half-hour of each other Friday afternoon, *both* sales cancelled. I was devastated; was there an evil conspiracy out to get me? No, it was just one of those things. Cancellations are part of a salesperson's reality—"them's the rules," my father used to say. There was nothing I could do except fly back to Spokane Sunday and begin anew. Spokane turned out to be a highly profitable town; the two cancellations were nothing more than a couple of ephemeral blemishes on an otherwise smooth complexion.

Keep Cancellations to a Minimum

My father was right: cancellations are part of the "rules"; but if you want to keep them to a minimum, you must *vigorously* post-close every time you make a sale. Post-closing is congratulating the buyer's astute judgment, and telling him how pleased he's going to be that he made the right decision.

Here's how I did it. Adapt to fit your business:

"Tony, you made a great decision, congratulations. If you're like most of our plumbing clients around the country, you're going to really be glad you're the plumbing contractor on our program. We're going to have a tremendous impact on the business in Spokane, and you're going to benefit greatly from that impact." Often I would tell him about letters we received from businesses we *didn't* call on, upset that *they* weren't offered the space, because *they* were the best plumbing company in town and *should have been contacted first*!

I wanted my client to feel intelligent, special, and fortunate. I also wanted to cover him in protective armor, in case a friend or family member ridiculed his decision to buy our advertising.

"You bought *what*!? Are you out of your mind!? Ted Bear bought 'something like that' and told me it was the dumbest thing he ever did. You better cancel before it's too late!"

A smart salesperson knows post-closing is an integral part of the sale. She would no more omit it than try to present without her visual aid, contract, and pen. I suggest you look at it in the same light. If you don't, you'll regret it when the cancellations start raining down on you.

Unless you think jumping two feet off the ground like a frog every time the phone rings sounds like a lot of fun and good exercise…

56
Technology

"Information technology and business are becoming inextricably interwoven. I don't think anybody can talk meaningfully about one without talking about the other."

Bill Gates

My three magnificent children—42, 38, and 29—are so computer savvy I truly am in awe. I, on the other hand, struggle with technology, typical of my generation. My older son, Michael (Michael does communications and public relations for the Buffalo Grove Park District, is a trustee of that village, former weekend public-address announcer for the Chicago Cubs, and last but not least, father of my grandson, Jack) has come over numerous times to rescue me because I did *something*—God only knows what—to shipwreck the manuscript of this book.

Thank you, Michael!

Other than writing letters, sending e-mails, and watching my wife get the company books ready on Excel for Dave Levinson, my selling career was devoid of technology. I know, though, that Facebook, Twitter, LinkedIn, and other social-networking sites are a must for today's modern salesperson. We've all read stories regarding technology and the Internet that exhort the salesperson to "get with it."

I retired from sales before I had to "get with it," but my writing and speaking career has necessitated that I "get with it": I now have a website and use Facebook, Twitter, and LinkedIn. Necessity still is the mother of invention…

…and adaptability is the hallmark of a master salesperson *and* a writer/speaker.

So get with it! If someone my age can do it, so can you.

Remember, though, these are only tools. It's easier to be a good gardener with the right tools, but it's still *you* who has to do the planting, cultivating, and harvesting.

57

Greatness

"I believe that everyone has
the potential for Greatness."

Robert Terson

On my 60th birthday Barry Thalden sent me a gift I'll treasure till the day I die—a single framed set of portraits of us in our 20s, attired in tuxedos, along with the above quote.

We all have the potential for Greatness. Remember, life will give you whatever you demand of it. If, as a salesperson, you demand the moon and the stars and all else that glitters and shines, they're yours for the taking. All you need is the desire to want it enough, the belief in yourself to go after it, and the strength of character to hang in there when the Devil comes after you with his shaker of discouragement. That and the knowledge I've shared with you.

That's all there is to it.

So, this time with a glass of Dom Pérignon in my hand: here's to your future as a master salesperson, and to living the sweet life… on your own terms.

About the Author

Robert Terson has been a sales professional and entrepreneur his entire adult life. He retired from his advertising company, after 38 years of being in business, in January 2010 to begin a second career as a writer and speaker. He resides in Arlington Heights, Illinois and is the founder and CEO of Sellingfearlessly.com. He invites you to contact him at that site or email him at Robert@sellingfearlessly.com.